The Entrepreneur PAPA's Secrets #4

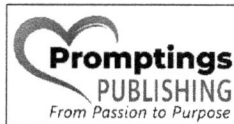

Promptings
PUBLISHING
From Passion to Purpose

May You Have

Enough happiness to keep you *sweet,*

Enough trials to keep you *strong,*

Enough sorrow to keep you *human,*

Enough hope to keep you *happy,*

Enough failure to keep you *humble,*

Enough success to keep you *eager,*

Enough friends to give you *comfort,*

Enough wealth to meet your *needs,*

Enough enthusiasm to look *forward,*

Enough faith to banish *depression,*

Enough determination to make each day

better than *yesterday.*

(Author Unknown)

Aloha! From beautiful Hawaii!

David Selley

Dedication

To Visionaries Who Inspire

Great achievements often stem from unwavering determination, innovative thinking, and a bold refusal to settle for the ordinary. This book is dedicated to two leaders whose journeys embody these ideals, inspiring us to think bigger, dream brighter, and forge paths to a better future.

Donald Trump

As an entrepreneur and now as President, you've shown us the power of resilience, ambition, and standing firm in the face of challenges. Your journey reminds us that no dream is too big, and no setback too great, to be overcome with vision and strength. I admire your ability to lead with conviction and your unwavering drive to turn bold ideas into reality, inspiring countless others to pursue their own paths.

Elon Musk

Your relentless pursuit of the extraordinary—whether in business or as a co-chair in efforts to enhance government efficiency—has changed what we believe is possible. You've shown us that real innovation comes from daring to explore the unknown and thinking beyond limits. I am inspired by your commitment to progress and your unique vision for a better future. Your work is a testament to the boundless potential of human ingenuity and passion.

Foreword

Papa the Entrepreneur

Webster's dictionary defines an entrepreneur as "one who organizes, manages, and assumes the risk of a business or enterprise." I can think of no one who fits that description better than David. As you'll discover in this chapter, David has walked the walk and talked the talk, unlike some "professionals" who have never even started or owned their own business. If you've ever had a brilliant idea but let it drift off your mental landscape, this chapter will guide you through simple steps to break free. Maybe you've been frustrated with the many restrictions in your life, or perhaps you wanted to step out of your comfort zone but were too scared. If that's the case, this chapter is for you. It's filled with experiences that demonstrate the "can-do" attitude every entrepreneur must have to follow their dreams and achieve their goals.

I know because I'm also an entrepreneur.

It was the early 80s, and I was fresh out of the Navy SEALs after Grenada, honorably discharged. I ended up in Carpinteria, California with my brother in a condo we couldn't afford. Someone invited me to a networking meeting where David was the guest speaker. I dressed my best, and afterward, David zeroed in on me. Maybe it was my three-piece suit, gold watch, or new shoes—I don't know why, but we've been friends ever since.

After a few one-on-one conversations, David and his wife, Sonja, realized our circumstances when we couldn't pay the rent. I'll always be grateful to them for opening their home to my brother and me in Westlake Village. Sonja, like a second mom, showed us love while we devoured her delicious meals. Soon, David helped me get a job as a diesel mechanic at the local trash company. Returning home each night covered in grease didn't sit well with Sonja's neat housekeeping. One night at dinner, David changed my life with his words: "Larry!... You're too smart to be a grease monkey for the rest of your life. Use your brains, not your brawn, and work for yourself." He helped me prepare a sales resume, and within two weeks, I was hired as a salesman for a fastener company in Southern California.

Then came another life-changing moment: David and Sonja invited me to their church, where I met my wife, Dianna, at a singles group. We married soon after, with David and Sonja in attendance. Dianna, a recent graduate in mechanical engineering, studied the product I sold and said she could design a better one—more effective, efficient, and cost-friendly. We formed Sealtight Fasteners, got a U.S. patent, and landed a NASA contract. Our product is now the only rivet of its kind on the Lunar Lander, which brought us world- wide recognition and business.

Unfortunately, another company stole our patent, leading to an 18-year legal battle. It cost us several hundred thousand dollars, but we won a 7-2 decision in our favor at the U.S. Supreme Court on December 8th, 2014.

David and Sonja have supported us through thick and thin. It's comforting to know you have someone in your corner when you need them.

As published authors, David wrote the foreword to our book *The Theory of Reality*. Now, we return the favor with pride. As you read this chapter, you'll understand why we're honored to call David and Sonja our friends. Entrepreneurs often seem like misfits because they have the courage to step out of conformity and stretch beyond their comfort zones.

We know you'll learn much from this book.

Larry & Dianna Bogatz
Santa Barbara, California

"David Selley's PAPA Book Series: A Guinness World Record Journey" The PAPA Book Series

(Part of a Guinness World Record Attempt: "The Oldest Author to Publish the Most Books in One Year")

David Selley's *PAPA Book Series* is an extraordinary collection of life stories, lessons, and wisdom, part of his bold attempt to set a Guinness World Record as the **oldest author to publish the most books in a single year**. The series spans David's journey across **three continents**— as a son, father, entrepreneur, and husband—offering readers a rich tapestry of memoir and practical advice, rooted in personal experience.

At the heart of this series is not only David's vast entrepreneurial experience but also the story of his 65-year marriage, a remarkable testament to the power of love, perseverance, and partnership. Throughout the books, David reflects on how his marriage shaped his personal and professional life, offering readers invaluable lessons on building and sustaining long-lasting relationships, as seen in *PAPA #6: The Four Seasons of Marriage* and *PAPA #7: How to Stay Married 65+ Years*. His insights will resonate with anyone looking to navigate the evolving phases of life with grace and commitment.

Additionally, as David transitions into his latest entrepreneurial project, the series introduces readers to the potential benefits of his International Entrepreneur Association (IEA), which aims to foster a global import/export network. This network will create exciting new opportunities for businesses worldwide, facilitated by Executive Directors in each of the top 20 countries. By leveraging his extensive knowledge and global connections, David envisions a closed system where importers and exporters can trade efficiently, creating a new revenue stream for IEA members. This groundbreaking initiative highlights how modern entrepreneurship can cross borders, providing financial growth and networking opportunities for businesses and entrepreneurs alike.

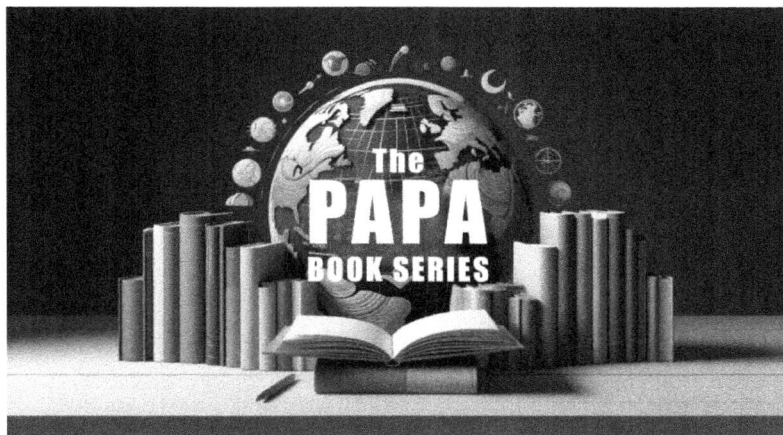

SERIES TITLES AVAILABLE NOW:

PAPA #1: The Boy in England and Growing Up Tough is a tale of resilience and survival from David's early days in England.

PAPA #2: The Young Man in Canada provides a look at his transformative years in Canada, filled with personal and professional growth.

PAPA #3: The Businessman and Entrepreneur in the USA chronicles David's entry into the business world and his entrepreneurial adventures in the United States.

PAPA #4: The Entrepreneur: PAPAS Secret #4 takes a deep dive into his entrepreneurial mindset and the lessons learned from building businesses.

Continued on next page

TITLES COMING SOON:

PAPA #5: Three Lives, Three Lands
A condensed journey through David Selley's life in England, Canada, and the USA

PAPA #6: Married – The Four Seasons of Marriage reflects on the evolving phases of marriage over 65+ years, from spring to winter.

PAPA #7: How Is Your Relationship? (How to Stay Married 65+ Years)

PAPA #8: The Father explores David's journey as a father, filled with challenges, love, and important lessons.

PAPA #9: The Grandfather – Leaving a Legacy is a heartwarming tribute to family and the importance of passing down wisdom and values.

PAPA #10: Health, Wealth & Happiness (You Can Have All Three)
is a guide to achieving balance and abundance in life.

PAPA #11: The Investor – Nothing Down Real Estate...
Yes! It Works presents proven strategies for real estate investing without upfront costs.

PAPA #12: The Famous 50 Book Series is an exciting global vanity publishing project, connecting famous people across industries at *www.famous50.com*.

TABLE OF CONTENTS

TABLE OF CONTENTS - continued

RECOMMENDED READING

Insights and Reflections:
Keys to Entrepreneurial Success

TABLE OF CONTENTS - continued

The Entrepreneur!

"I aspire to inspire before I expire"
David Selley

The Journey Begins

Entrepreneurship is a journey — one that's thrilling, unpredictable, and deeply personal. Over my lifetime, I've taken this journey across three continents, from the bustling markets of England to the vast opportunities of Canada and the United States. Along the way, I've started ventures that flourished and others that failed spectacularly. But through it all, I've learned lessons that have shaped who I am today and the values I hold dear.

One principle has guided me throughout my life: 'I aspire to inspire before I expire.' It's a phrase I coined to remind myself of the importance of sharing what I've learned to help others. Looking back now, I often think....

'If I knew then what I know now..."

...how much smoother might the path have been?' That thought has been the driving force behind this book.

This book is more than just a collection of stories. At the end of each venture, you'll find tools to help you engage with the lessons shared in that chapter. Reflection questions encourage you to pause and consider how the insights apply to your own journey. Practical takeaways provide actionable advice to help you move forward in your entrepreneurial endeavors. Whether you're just starting out or you've been in business for years, this book is designed to guide, challenge, and support you.

So, as you turn the pages, think of this as more than a book—it's a companion for your entrepreneurial adventure. I invite you to join me on this journey, not just to learn about mine, but to grow through your own.

– David Selley

> "Success isn't measured only by
> the ventures we build,
> but also by the wisdom we share
> and the people we empower
> to build their own."
>
> - David Selley

Is Entrepreneurship Right for You?

Reveal Your Readiness
With this Self Evaluation
Opportunity

Entrepreneurship is a journey that will test every part of who you are. The following 20 questions I'm sharing with you aren't just checkpoints, they're tools to help you dig deep, uncover blind spots, and recognize opportunities you might otherwise miss. Answer each one honestly. Take your time. Let these questions reveal where you're thriving and where you might need to adjust. Consider it your personal evaluation, a chance to step back and see your path more clearly. This isn't just about business; it's about building a life that aligns with who you truly are and the impact you want to make.

I designed these questions to help you assess your readiness and mindset for the entrepreneurial journey. Rate yourself on a scale from 1 to 10, with 1 meaning 'I struggle with this' and 10 meaning 'I feel very confident.' Be honest—this is a tool for insight, not judgment, to reveal your strengths and areas for growth. Take your time and reflect; your answers will guide you in understanding your preparedness and areas to focus on as you move forward.

Self-Evaluation: Answer Each Question on a Scale of 1 to 10

1. **How strongly do I feel about being an entrepreneur?** Clarify your motivations— are they driven by passion, freedom, financial gain, or something else?

   1 2 3 4 5 6 7 8 9 10 (___)

2. **Am I comfortable with uncertainty and risk?** Entrepreneurship often involves stepping into the unknown; are you ready for that?

   1 2 3 4 5 6 7 8 9 10 (___)

3. **Can I handle financial instability, especially in the early stages?** Most businesses take time to become profitable. Are you prepared for fluctuating income?

   1 2 3 4 5 6 7 8 9 10 (___)

4. **Do I have a problem-solving mindset?** Entrepreneurs face constant challenges. Can you find solutions, or do obstacles make you back down?

   1 2 3 4 5 6 7 8 9 10 (___)

5. **How do I handle failure?** Failure is a significant part of learning in entrepreneurship. Can you bounce back and keep going after setbacks?

   1 2 3 4 5 6 7 8 9 10 (___)

6. **Am I able to work independently and stay self-motivated?** In the early days, you're responsible for all aspects of the business. Can you motivate yourself?

   1 2 3 4 5 6 7 8 9 10 (___)

7. **Can I accept feedback and criticism without taking it personally?** Entrepreneurship requires resilience. Can you use criticism constructively?

   1 2 3 4 5 6 7 8 9 10 (___)

8. **Do I have a support system (family, friends, or mentors) to lean on?** A strong support network can help you weather the tough times.

   1 2 3 4 5 6 7 8 9 10 ( )

9. **Am I willing to work long hours and make personal sacrifices?** Are you ready to commit significant time and effort?

   1 2 3 4 5 6 7 8 9 10 ( )

10. **Do I have the patience to wait for success?** Are you prepared to stay patient and consistent?

   1 2 3 4 5 6 7 8 9 10 ( )

11. **How do I handle stress and pressure?**
Can you stay calm, focused, and productive in high-stress situations?

1   2   3   4   5   6   7   8   9   10   (   )

12. **Am I adaptable and open to change?** The business landscape can change quickly. Can you pivot when needed?

1   2   3   4   5   6   7   8   9   10   (___)

13. **Do I have a unique idea or skill set that solves a real problem?** Are you offering something that people need or want?

1   2   3   4   5   6   7   8   9   10   (   )

14. **Can I communicate my vision and goals effectively?** You need to articulate your ideas clearly, whether to clients, investors, or team members.

1   2   3   4   5   6   7   8   9   10   (   )

15. **Am I ready to learn continuously?** The business world is always evolving. Are you committed to ongoing learning?

1   2   3   4   5   6   7   8   9   10   (   )

16. **Can I manage money effectively?** Financial management is crucial. Can you budget and track spending accurately?

1   2   3   4   5   6   7   8   9   10   (   )

17. **Am I comfortable with networking and building relationships?** Entrepreneurship is often about who you know. Are you willing to network.

    1 2 3 4 5 6 7 8 9 10 (   )

18. **Do I understand my target market?** Knowing your audience is critical. Do you understand who you're serving and what they need?

    1 2 3 4 5 6 7 8 9 10 (   )

19. **Am I willing to take responsibility for all decisions and outcomes?** As the boss, success and failure both rest on your shoulders. Can you handle the accountability?

    1 2 3 4 5 6 7 8 9 10 (   )

20. **Can I see myself doing this for years, even if success takes longer than expected?** Entrepreneurship is a long-term journey. Do you have the passion and patience to stay the course?

    1 2 3 4 5 6 7 8 9 10 (   )

    Overall Self-Evaluation Score   (   )

Now that you've added up your score, take a moment to reflect on what it reveals about your entrepreneurial readiness. This total gives you a snapshot of your current strengths and areas for growth.

You're well-prepared   **You're on the right path**   **Build your readiness**

- **160–200**: You're well-prepared for the entrepreneurial journey! You have a strong foundation, and with continued focus, you're likely ready to tackle the challenges ahead.

- **100–159**: You're on the right path, but there are a few areas where growth could make your journey smoother. Use this insight to focus on the skills or mindsets that could help you feel more confident.

- **Below 100**: This may indicate that you have some work to do before fully diving into entrepreneurship. Consider exploring resources, mentorship, or further reflection to build the readiness and resilience you need.

Remember, this score isn't a final verdict but a tool to guide your growth. Entrepreneurship is a journey of learning and adapting, and every step forward is progress.

> "The first step to entrepreneurship is knowing yourself.
> The second is daring to try."
>
> - David Selley

Lessons That Stand the Test of Time

Every lesson learned in entrepreneurship is like a seed planted in the mind. Some grow into lifelong principles, while others fade, overtaken by new challenges. But the ones that stand the test of time are the ones rooted in truth, resilience, and experience. What are these timeless lessons, and how can they guide your journey?

The insights ahead aren't flashy tricks or the kind of quick hacks you might find in a trending social media post. They don't promise overnight success, nor do they fade with the latest digital trend. Instead, what you'll find here is enduring wisdom—a toolkit that has guided me, David Selley, through decades of entrepreneurial ventures across England, Canada, and the United States. These principles have weathered every challenge, adapting to new landscapes and proving their value time and again.

Unlike social media sound bites that catch your attention and disappear just as quickly, these lessons have depth.

They aren't about surface-level wins but about building a foundation for sustainable growth and long-term success. You may encounter recurring themes—focus, resilience, financial discipline, and learning from setbacks—and each instance is a testament to the power of these ideas when applied with intention. Real wisdom isn't in one-off tricks; it's in principles that stand the test of time, reshaping themselves to meet new challenges and emerging stronger with every evolution.

These are not static ideas—they're flexible and incredibly relevant for our fast-paced, digital age. The value lies in understanding how these foundational principles, proven over time, can be adapted and applied in new ways, giving you a solid ground to navigate an ever-changing world.

Yes, you may find some ideas repeated across different ventures, contexts, or challenges, but don't skim over them. Instead, look at each repetition as a reminder of their importance. Real wisdom isn't in a single instance; it's in the recurring truths that show up time and again, proving their value across vastly different scenarios.

Think About This
- What is one principle you've carried with you throughout your career or life? How has it served you?
- Have you ever abandoned a lesson, only to realize later that it was still valuable?
- How do you distinguish between advice worth keeping and advice to leave behind?

How Would This Apply to You?

- Write down a single lesson from your past that you believe is timeless. How can you apply it today?
- Reflect on one failure or challenge that taught you something invaluable. How has that lesson shaped your decisions since?
- Consider someone you respect as a mentor or guide. What is one piece of advice from them that continues to resonate with you?

"Timeless lessons don't just teach us what to do—
they teach us who we are." – David Selley

Procrastination

The Price of Procrastination

Time waits for no one, and neither does opportunity.
Procrastination may feel harmless in the moment, but the price
it exacts is steep. What has delaying cost you, and how can you
reclaim the time and opportunities you've lost?

There's a saying that "the most expensive real estate in the world is the graveyard," filled with unwritten books, unbuilt businesses, It's a place where millions of dreams, untapped talents, and unrealized potential lie buried. How many world-changing ideas have gone to the grave simply because someone hesitated too long or doubted themselves? Procrastination is a thief, robbing people not only of time but of the life they might have lived. It's a stark reminder of the high cost of inaction, where ideas are buried, never seeing the light of day.

Procrastination, whether due to fear, uncertainty, or lack of guidance, is often the invisible barrier that keeps great potential locked away.

Procrastination might be a quiet adversary, but it's one that every entrepreneur faces at some point. It holds people back, convincing them that they'll have time later, that maybe the idea isn't ready, or that someone else can do it better. But successful entrepreneurs learn to fight procrastination—not by sheer willpower alone, but by finding people who can guide, support, and challenge them.

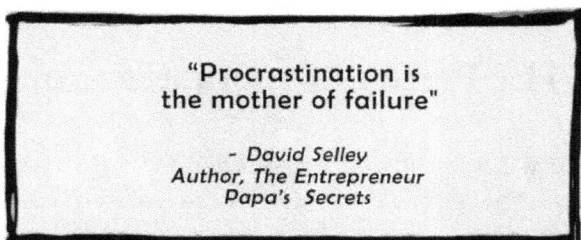

> "Procrastination is the mother of failure"
>
> *- David Selley*
> *Author, The Entrepreneur Papa's Secrets*

Think About This
- When have you delayed taking action on an idea or decision? What was the result?

- How do you typically prioritize tasks and projects? Does procrastination play a role?
- What fears or doubts contribute to your hesitation when starting something new

How Would This Apply to You?
- Identify one task or project you've been putting off. Commit to starting it today.
- Reflect on the emotional or mental blocks that lead you to procrastinate. What can you do to overcome them?
- Create a daily habit of tackling the most challenging task on your list first.

"The cost of delay isn't just time lost—
it's progress, potential and
peace of mind."

- *David Selley*
Entrepreneur, Author

Mentorship

The Antidote to Procrastination

This is where mentorship becomes invaluable. A mentor doesn't just offer advice; they help others move beyond hesitation, transforming doubts into actionable plans. They reveal blind spots, encourage calculated risks, and provide insights only experience can offer. Good mentorship doesn't just prepare someone for success; it pushes them past their excuses and into their potential.

> "A true mentor
> doesn't just show the way—
> they inspire you to
> carve your own path."
>
> - David Selley
> Entrepreneur, Author

What Does Success Look Like?

"Success is a tricky word. When I was 11, selling stamps felt like success—coins in my pocket and a bit of independence. But as I took on new ventures, my idea of success kept evolving. Real success is more than what you see in movies; it's about creating something meaningful, finding fulfillment, and having the resilience to keep going."

The Real Version of Success: More Than Just the Wins

"Success isn't about never failing. Some of my best lessons came from ventures that didn't work out, like The Gourmet Chalet. I learned about timing and the importance of preparation. Real success is about growth, even if things don't go as planned."

Success is Found in Purpose, Not Just Profits
"Ask yourself, 'Why am I doing this?' If the answer is just 'to make money,' it'll be hard to stick with it. With Sonja's

Food & Gifts, I wanted to create a joyful space, not just turn a profit. Purpose makes success more fulfilling."

Resilience is the Secret Ingredient of Success
"Success doesn't happen overnight. Some ventures took years to pay off, and others didn't. When Sure Safe Auto Device didn't work out, I didn't let it stop me. Resilience—getting back up and trying again—is what success looks like."

The Importance of Impact:
Who Benefits from Your Success?
"Success isn't just about you; it's about who benefits. Senior Parks USA wasn't just a business; it was about giving people a safe place to live. True success is more rewarding when it impacts others."

Success is Never Static –
It's a Journey of Continuous Growth
"Success isn't a final destination. When I completed 22 'nothing down' real estate deals, I thought I'd hit my peak. But true success is about growing and taking on new challenges."

Defining Success for Yourself
"Society has all kinds of definitions for success, but only yours matters. Real success is fulfilling and often hard-earned. It's found in resilience, impact, and personal growth. Define it for yourself, and every step forward will feel like a win."

A Note to the New Entrepreneur
"Don't chase someone else's version of success. Build

your own. Success may not always be clear in the moment, but with purpose, resilience, and impact, it will find you."

Key Takeaways

- Success is about growth, not just wins.
- Purpose makes success lasting.
- Resilience is essential for overcoming setbacks.
- Impact matters: true success benefits others.
- Success is an evolving journey, not a destination.

Think About This

- How do you define success in your life right now? Has that definition changed over time?
- When have you achieved something you once thought defined success, only to realize it wasn't fulfilling?
- What do you think makes success sustainable, not just achievable?

How Would This Apply to You?

- Write down three aspects of success that matter most to you (e.g., impact, freedom, financial stability).
- Reflect on one area where your definition of success could align better with your personal values.
- Think about a long-term goal. What small steps can you take this week to move closer to it?

> "Success isn't about standing
> on one pillar—
> it's about building a foundation
> strong enough to hold your dreams."
>
> - David Selley

18 Pillars of Success

What defines success? For every entrepreneur, the answer is different, but the pillars that support it are often universal. These principles are the foundation of lasting achievement, and they hold the secrets to navigating both the challenges and triumphs of building a business. Which pillars will you choose to strengthen your journey?

Success isn't just about talent or luck; it's built on proven principles that foster momentum, resilience, and sustainable growth. These 18 Pillars of Success are timeless because they align with the core elements of achievement: clarity, consistency, adaptability, and determination. When applied, they form a powerful foundation that helps you overcome obstacles, maximize opportunities, and stay focused on what truly matters. Think of these as the essential building blocks for lasting success—each one designed to strengthen your path, keep you moving forward, and bring you closer to achieving your ultimate goals..

1. Set Clear, Attainable Goals

Success begins with clarity. Define what you want to achieve in specific, measurable terms to give your efforts direction and focus.

2. Take Consistent Action

The difference between dreams and reality is action. Make a habit of taking steps toward your goals every day, even when motivation wanes.

3. Embrace Lifelong Learning

Success is a continuous journey. Commit to learning new skills, staying updated, and adapting to changes in your field.

4. Build a Strong Network

Success rarely happens in isolation. Cultivate relationships with mentors, peers, and other professionals who can support and inspire you.

5. Develop Resilience

Challenges are inevitable; build resilience by turning setbacks into growth opportunities.

6. Manage Time Effectively

Time is your most valuable resource. Prioritize tasks, set

deadlines, and use tools to stay organized and focused on high-impact activities.

7. Stay Adaptable

Flexibility allows you to respond to unexpected changes and seize new opportunities. Be open to adjusting your strategies as needed.

8. Focus on Solutions, Not Problems

Successful people are solution oriented. Instead of dwelling on obstacles, focus on finding ways to overcome them and move forward.

9. Invest in Self-Care

Physical and mental well-being are foundational to success. Prioritize health, rest, and stress management to maintain peak performance.

10. Cultivate a Positive Mindset

A positive attitude fosters creativity and per- severance. Approach challenges with optimism and surround your-self with encouraging influences.

11. Work with Integrity

Build trust by acting with honesty and transparency. Integrity attracts loyalty, respect, and long-term success.

12. Set and Uphold Boundaries

Protect time energy by setting clear boundaries, both in personal and professional areas, to prevent burnout and focus.

13. Seek Constructive Feedback

Growth comes from constructive input. Be open to feedback and use it to improve your performance and refine your approach.

14. Delegate Wisely

Recognize that you can't do everything alone. Delegate tasks to free up time for what you do best and to help others grow.

15. Prepare, Empower & Achieve

Preparation boosts confidence. Know your material, practice your skills, and be ready for the challenges you anticipate.

16. Practice Financial Discipline

Effective money management is essential for long-term success. Save, budget, and invest wisely to secure your future.

17. ■ Stay Passionate and Purpose-Driven

Purpose fuels perseverance. Aligning your work with your values and passions, and let that drive sustain you through challenges.

18. ■ Celebrate Small Wins

Acknowledge progress, even if it's minor. Celebrating small victories keeps you motivated and reinforces positive habits.

Think About This
- Which of these pillars do you feel you've already mastered? Which needs more attention?
- How do your personal values align with the pillars of success?
- When have you seen these principles play out in someone else's success story? What did you learn?

How Would This Apply to You?
- Pick one pillar you feel is weakest in your own life or business. Write down three steps you can take to strengthen it.
- Reflect on how these principles align with your long-term goals. What adjustments can you make to better align with them?
- Share one of these pillars with a colleague or mentee and discuss how they can apply it in their journey.

Success isn't a destination—
it's the result of a strong
foundation built over time.

Discover 18 principles that
guide growth,
overcome challenges,
and drive lasting success.

18 Success Strategies for the Modern Entrepreneur

"Strategies are the roadmap to success. Without them, even the best intentions can fail. These 18 strategies aren't just steps—they're principles to guide you through challenges, seize opportunities, and build a future worth striving for. How will you make them yours?"

1.

How to Overcome Self-Limiting Beliefs and Unlock Creativity

Challenge the beliefs holding you back by identifying one area where you feel stuck, and question if those limitations are truly real. Practice reframing doubts into possibilities, expose yourself to fresh ideas and diverse cultures to fuel creativity.

2.

How to Pivot Your Business Strategy When the Market Shifts

When the landscape changes, study the trends and ask, "What's the new demand?" Test small adjustments in your offerings to see what sticks. Flexibility lets you meet market needs head-on, helping you turn disruptions into opportunities.

3.

How to Build a Resilient Entrepreneurial Mindset

Resilience is built by facing challenges. Start by reframing setbacks as part of your growth, not as failures. Develop routines that support mental strength, like daily reflection or mindfulness, so you can handle any obstacle with clarity and confidence.

4.

How to Turn Failure into Opportunity

After any setback, take time to analyze what went wrong without self-blame. Ask, "What can I improve, and what can I leverage?" Turn each lesson into a strategic move forward, building on what you've learned to refine your approach.

5.

How to Create a Mission-Driven Business with Long-Term Impact

Define a purpose that goes beyond profit, connecting with values that matter to you and your audience. Ask yourself, "What do I want to change in the world?" Use this mission to drive decisions and inspire your team and customers alike.

6.

How to Build Systems for Scalability and Consistency

To scale successfully, document your processes step-by-step. Automate what you can and create standards so that growth doesn't sacrifice quality. This allows your business to expand smoothly, with every step strengthening the brand.

7.

How to Identify and Solve Real Problems
in the Market

Identify customer pain points and market gaps. Understand the "why" behind each problem and create solutions that meet those needs. This keeps your product or service in demand.

8.

How to Navigate Financial Setbacks
and Thrive

Build a financial buffer and diversify your revenue streams to stay steady during downturns. Track your spending closely and cut unnecessary costs without impacting quality. Strategic financial management allows you to weather any storm.

9.

How to Build Trust and Strong
Relationship with Customers

Trust is earned through consistency and integrity. Engage with your customers regularly, show transparency in all communications, and follow up on promises. Small actions—like responding quickly to concerns—build a solid foundation of trust that enhances customer loyalty.

10.

How to Set Effective Goals and Track Progress

Begin with clear, specific goals that align with your business vision. Break these down into measurable milestones and use tools to track your progress. Regularly review and adjust as needed, ensuring each goal continues to serve your broader objectives.

11.

How to Leverage Networking for Growth

Networking isn't just about meeting people; it's about building mutually beneficial relationships. Approach networking with the mindset of offering value first, whether it's a referral, advice, or support. This creates a network that's supportive and rewarding, driving growth over time.

12.

How to Manage Time Efficiently as an Entrepreneur

Time is your most valuable asset. Use prioritization techniques like the Eisenhower Matrix (urgent vs. important tasks) and consider time-blocking for focused work sessions. Regularly review how your time is spent and adjust to ensure productivity aligns with your goals.

13.

How to Embrace Technology to Enhance Business Operations

Identify areas where technology can improve your business, such as customer service, marketing, or operations. Use tools to automate tasks, streamline processes, and enhance data tracking, freeing you for strategic work.

14.

How to Make Data-Driven Decisions

Gather relevant data on customer preferences, market trends, and business performance. Use analytics tools to interpret this data and base your decisions on concrete insights rather than guesses. Data-driven decisions increase your chances of achieving desired outcomes.

15.

How to Create a Strong Brand Identity

Define what your brand stands for, including its core values, tone, and visual style. Ensure consistency in every touch-point, from your website to social media. A strong brand identity builds recognition and fosters loyalty among your audience.

16.

How to Stay Ahead of Industry Trends
Stay informed by following industry news, attending webinars, and joining networks. Watch for trends and assess their impact on your business. Staying up-to-date helps you adapt and remain competitive.

17.

How to Foster a Collaborative Team Culture

Foster open communication, feedback, and teamwork. Set shared goals, celebrate achievements, and offer growth opportunities. A collaborative culture motivates your team and boosts your business.

18.

How to Balance Work and Life for Sustainable Success

Set boundaries for work hours and protect personal time. Practice self-care, delegate tasks when possible, and create a schedule that includes downtime. Sustainable success comes from a balanced approach, preventing burnout and keeping you energized.

> "What separates the winners from the losers is how a person reacts to each new twist of fate."
>
> *- Donald Trump*
> *45th and 47th President of the United States*
> *Chairman and President of the Trump Organization*

The Entrepreneur's DNA:

Are You Wired to Thrive in the Unexpected?

Do you love solving problems, even the ones you didn't see coming?

If you see challenges as puzzles waiting to be solved, not disasters in the making, then you're already thinking like an entrepreneur! Bonus points if your response to a problem is 'Bring it on!' rather than 'Why me?!' But remember, not all problems come with a manual— sometimes you have to get creative, think on your feet, and yes, even make it up as you go!

Can you turn a "no" into "not yet", or do you give up after the first no?

"Entrepreneurs hear 'no' a lot, but the real pros know it's just part of the game. If your first instinct is to reframe 'no' as 'not yet,' you're already ahead of the pack! Think of it as the universe testing your resolve. The more doors that close, the closer you are to finding one that opens. Remember, persistence is key, and sometimes, success is just one more 'not yet' away!"

Are you okay with uncertainty, or do you need a GPS for every step of the journey?

"If you're the kind of person who can handle a little (or a lot) of unpredictability, you're built for entrepreneurship! Sure, it's nice to know where you're headed, but sometimes the journey is full of twists, turns, and detours. The best entrepreneurs thrive in chaos, turning unknowns into opportunities. So, do you need a perfect map, or are you ready to explore uncharted territory with just a compass and a hunch?"

How do you feel about mistakes?
Are they learning time or panic time?

Mistakes are part of the entrepreneurial adventure! Do you see them as chances to learn or reasons to panic? Successful entrepreneurs view mistakes as stepping-stones to growth. When things go wrong, do you ask, 'How can I fix this?' or look for an exit? Remember, each mistake holds a lesson in growth.

Do you have a wild idea right now that's been sitting in the back of your mind, waiting for its moment?

"Every great entrepreneur has at least one wild idea that they can't shake off. It's that 'what if' thought that keeps popping up, just waiting for the right time to shine. Maybe it's quirky, maybe it's bold, but it's yours. Successful entrepreneurs know when to bring that idea forward and give it life. So, what's your wild idea? Is it time to dust it off and let it run free, or will it stay in the 'someday' folder a little longer?"

How do you handle stress – meditation or by making a to-do list at 2 a.m.?

"Stress is inevitable in entrepreneurship, but how you handle it makes all the difference! Are you the type to stay calm with deep breaths and meditation, or are you up at 2 a.m. scribbling down a to-do list like your life depends on it? Whether you find your zen or thrive on that late-night adrenaline, successful entrepreneurs find a way to channel stress into productivity. So, what's your go-to method: peaceful meditation or midnight planning sessions?"

When things get tough, do you pivot like a pro or get stuck in the same place?

"Entrepreneurship isn't a straight line—it's more like a dance, and sometimes you have to pivot! When the going gets tough, do you adapt and find new ways forward, or do you freeze up like a deer in headlights? Great entrepreneurs know how to shift gears, change direction, and turn obstacles into opportunities. So, when life throws you a curveball, are you ready to pivot like a pro, or are you still staring at that dead-end road?"

Can you balance ambition with patience, or do you want success... like, yesterday?

"Ambition is great—every entrepreneur needs a good dose of it—but can you balance it with a little patience? Or are you the type who wants results, like yesterday? Success takes time, and the best entrepreneurs know it's a marathon, not a sprint. So, can you nurture your big dreams while letting them grow, or are you refreshing your inbox every five minutes waiting for that breakthrough?"

Do you see competition as a motivator or a deal-breaker?

"Competition is everywhere in the entrepreneurial world, but how do you handle it? Does it light a fire under you and push you to be better, or does it make you want to throw in the towel? The best entrepreneurs thrive on competition — they see it as a chance to innovate and stand out. So, is competition your fuel for greatness, or is it a deal-breaker that makes you second-guess everything?"

Can you picture yourself celebrating a big win, or are you too focused on the next goal?

"Success is sweet, but do you take the time to celebrate those big wins, or are you already chasing the next goal? Entrepreneurs are always on the move, but it's important to stop and enjoy the victories along the way! Can you picture yourself popping the champagne, or is your mind too busy planning the next challenge? Remember, a little celebration fuels future success!"

> "Constantly think about how you
> could be doing things better
> and keep questioning yourself."
>
> *- Elon Musk*
>
> *CEO and Technoking of Tesla / CEO and CTO of SpaceX*
> *Co-Chair Dept. of Government Efficiency (DOGE)*

A Ten-Cent Lesson in Determination

Set in the Southwest of England, imagine for a moment the bleakness and darkness of the post-World War II era, with food rationing and shortages of everything — including love for a fatherless eleven-year-old boy. That boy was a proud new Boy Scout, and his crisp uniform matched his dreams of achieving King Scout status in record time. Groundless ambition, not yet tempered by life's realities, was the driving force—the genesis of a winner's heart. In our house, there was no heating; the freezing cold water, especially in winter, only added to the misery of our sparse existence.

At our weekly meetings, we eagerly awaited special announcements, and this week was no exception. After my promotion to patrol leader, an announcement was made we could qualify individually and collectively for a trip to France to participate in the World Boy Scout Jamboree. That year's summer was unusually hot, and we all knew the only way to earn enough money for the prized trip was to excel in the annual Bob-a-Job fundraiser. This event allowed Boy Scouts to solicit from friends, relatives, and anyone who would give a "bob" (equal to ten cents) in exchange for a job. We had to earn one hundred bob to qualify for the trip in less than a month. It was a daunting task but stimulated all the creative juices an eleven-year-old could muster up. This was my first lesson in creative marketing. Sparse existence and miserly citizenship ruled in England, making objectives tough to meet. Still, with wild abandon, we created a large list (sound familiar?) of every possible prospect. An aggressive plan was laid out, and the work began in earnest.

There were, to be sure, all the routine jobs: trash collection, lawn mowing, sweeping, storing, stacking, cutting wood, and brush hauling. Then there were the less glamorous jobs, the ones that remained undone due to ill health, status, laziness, or a dad still away or absent from home forever. I knew that reaching my goal would require intense effort, so niche marketing was born for me. My grandmother always told me that to be successful, you had to make your point of difference your point of advantage. Today, the marketing gurus call that your USP. I discovered that a local farmer had a job no one else would do, and I quickly volunteered. In one fell swoop, I discovered an opportunity I thought would propel me over the top toward my dream trip to France. The job? Cleaning out eight chicken houses. Scoop, coup, or poop—it made no difference to me.

The chicken houses were six feet wide, eight feet long, four feet high, with a tiny door at the end for feeding and cleaning. The challenge was that it had been a long time since any cleaning had been done, and each house was compacted with thirty inches of chicken manure. Several adjectives could describe this today, but back then, I was somewhere between ignorance, youth, eagerness, blind ambition, poor negotiating skills, a cheapskate farmer, and the honor I held high with the Boy Scout pledge. I was to miss the coveted prize trip to France by seven bob.

I dug hard and fast, I scraped with fury, I itched and scratched, but as hard and fast as I worked, it became obvious that the time deadline would come and go. In those days, you did not ask for credit—it was a social disgrace even to think about it. As the days went by, a disheartened eleven-year-old kept at it and finished the job, but it was too late. The end benefit for this deeply scarred youngster was to embed a lifelong goal of achievement.

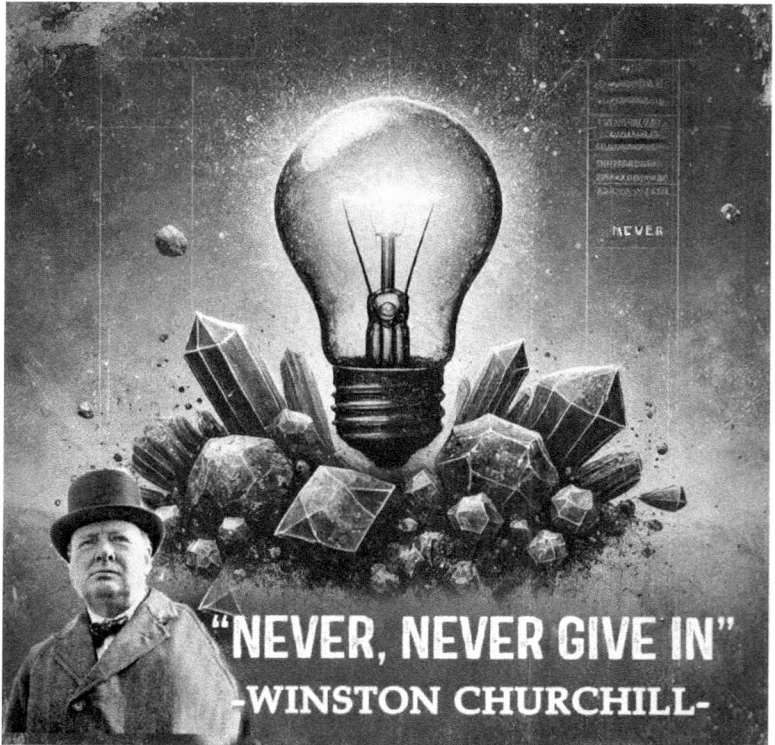

"NEVER, NEVER GIVE IN"
-WINSTON CHURCHILL-

Depth of Experience Versus Courage to Act

The following pages are the trials and lessons of 17 Entrepreneurial Ventures I have been involved in through the course of my life, along with a brief description of each. There are many more, but all began with an idea. The ideas that emerge from your fertile mind are like rough gems—useless until they are cleaned, polished, and tested for quality. The famous and shortest speech ever given by Sir Winston Churchill speaks volumes to entrepreneurs: "Never, never, never give in." He delivered that iconic line in 1941 when the situation in England looked bleak during the early stages of World War II.

#1 My First Business Venture:

Stamp Dealing at Age 11
(England, 1949)

Who would have thought that a simple fascination with stamps could uncover the secrets of trust and negotiation? At just 11 years old, David stumbled into a world where small mistakes carried big lessons— lessons that would shape the foundation of his entrepreneurial life.

My very first entrepreneurial venture was as a stamp dealer. At age eleven, I discovered—though not from school lessons—that if you bought something at one price and sold it for a higher price, you could make a profit. This realization was exhilarating because it meant I didn't have to beg for pocket money, which was scarce in those days. I've often thought that scarcity breeds ingenuity, and creativity follows. Using my active and creative skills, I found a way to start my stamp business with nothing down—a method I still use today in real estate transactions.

There was a "big-time" stamp dealer in a nearby town who shared my interest in philately. After a few conversations and a good character assessment on his part, he began loaning me collections of approval stamps without requiring cash up front. This process was based on trust, which I always honored, and it also gave me the chance to select stamps that aligned with the geography lessons we were studying in school. In today's business world, this would be called vertical and horizontal marketing.

Because I always seemed to have more pocket money than other kids, it didn't take long for my stamp business to attract attention at school. One day, while displaying my approval stamps during lunch, I realized that someone had stolen some of them. I knew exactly who it was. This led to a confrontation, and soon a schoolyard fight was underway. I was ready to fight for my principles — something I still do today.

Within minutes, the headmaster and PE teacher appeared as Brian and I punched and wrestled on the ground. Determined to get my stamps back, no matter the cost, we fought like it was mortal combat. Scraped, skinned, and bloody-nosed, we found ourselves at the feet of the entire school, still trying to land the final blow. We were stopped abruptly by the threat of expulsion—a family disgrace, personal humiliation, and the end to my already shaky academic record.

We both knew that fighting in the schoolyard meant severe punishment—detention at best, expulsion at worst. This didn't bother me much at the time, as I came from a fatherless home and secretly enjoyed the attention of being a "bad boy," even if it was for the wrong reasons. Defending my principles, however, was non-negotiable. How dare someone steal my stamps and claim ownership!

The punishment, delivered by our PE teacher, whom we affectionately called "Slug Meaden," was three one-minute rounds of boxing at the end of the next gym class, after our weekly five-mile run. Years earlier, one of our school's alumni, Teddy Walford, had become the British Army middleweight champion. He was a local hero, and Brian and I were eager to emulate him in our impending showdown.

We squared off with what looked like the largest boxing gloves I had ever seen—Everlast, of course. Little did I know that as soon as the leather started flying, the pain would follow. It didn't take long for me to realize I needed to give it my all—not just to win over my classmates, but to avoid getting clobbered. We sparred back and forth, likely looking ridiculous, as our pugilistic skills were nonexistent. The first round was even, with neither landing significant blows. By the second, we were already exhausted. By the third, we could barely lift our arms, flailing at each other in hopes of a lucky punch. The match was declared a draw.

Despite the fight, Brian and I became best friends. To this day, he swears he didn't steal my stamps, and, truthfully, it probably was someone else in the class. Changing someone's belief, though, is difficult until that "aha" moment arrives when you realize you were wrong. Brian forgave me for falsely accusing him, and we remained lifelong friends until his passing in 2016.

What I Learned

Operating in total economic ignorance but driven by ambition, I learned the basics of free enterprise—buy something at one price and sell it at another. I also learned the value of negotiating to the mutual benefit of both parties, and most importantly, the importance of keeping my word and maintaining integrity.

My biggest lesson was that trust is the foundation of any successful business. This early experience showed me that maintaining integrity and delivering on promises builds relationships that can last a lifetime.

Key Takeaways

At eleven years old, I didn't know much about business— except that buying low and selling high could earn me a bit of pocket money. But through that first venture, I learned more than just how to turn a profit. Here are the key lessons that stayed with me throughout my career:

Trust and Integrity
Are the Foundations of Business

When I started out as a stamp dealer, I didn't have the money to buy my stock upfront. Instead, I built a relationship of trust with a local dealer who allowed me to sell stamps on approval. That trust wasn't something I took lightly, and it was that commitment to honor my word that kept the door open for more opportunities. In every business, whether it's your first venture or your fiftieth, trust is the most valuable asset you have. Break that, and you're left with nothing.

Negotiation is a Skill You Must Master

It wasn't just about selling stamps; it was about creating mutual benefit. The dealer provided me with stamps, and I brought him customers. Negotiating to benefit both parties is critical. It's not about squeezing every penny but creating value for everyone involved. Whether you're new or seasoned, always approach negotiations with fairness. Long-lasting partnerships arise when everyone feels they've gained something.

Scarcity Breeds Ingenuity

Back then, I didn't have much money, but I didn't let that stop me. If anything, it pushed me to be more creative in how I approached business. When you have fewer resources, you learn to make the most of what you do have. It's the same principle today—don't wait for the perfect circumstances to start. Find ways to work within your limitations, and often, you'll uncover solutions that you wouldn't have seen otherwise.

Practical Advice for Modern Entrepreneurs

Trust is Key: Whether you're dealing with a supplier, a partner, or a customer, trust is essential. Build it, protect it, and never take it for granted. Without trust, your business relationships will crumble.

Embrace Scarcity: If you're low on resources, let that push you to think outside the box. Some of the best businesses start with very little but thrive on creative problem-solving.

Historical and Cultural Context

In 1949, England was still recovering from World War II. Resources were scarce, and many families, like mine, had to make do with less. This taught me resilience and resourcefulness. Nowadays, entrepreneurs have far more access to tools and resources, but the principles of ingenuity and grit are still the same. Don't let a lack of funding or resources deter you; often, the greatest ideas come out of necessity.

Inspiring Words

"Success is not final; failure is not fatal: It is the courage to continue that counts." — *Winston Churchill*

This quote always resonated with me. In business, just as in life, you'll face setbacks. But it's your ability to keep going that will set you apart.

Tie-In to Modern Entrepreneurial Challenges

In today's world, we live in a digital age where competition is fierce, and markets are global. However, the importance of trust, fair negotiation, and integrity remains unchanged. In fact, in a world of instant online reviews and social media visibility, maintaining trust is more critical than ever. My experience with stamps may seem small, but the principles of standing by your word, defending your values, and building lasting relationships are timeless. These are the pillars of long-term business success, even in today's fast-paced environment.

Community Building Tips

One unexpected outcome of my early business ventures was the community I built. From classmates to stamp dealers, I formed bonds based on mutual respect and shared interests. Never underestimate the power of community in your business journey. Surround yourself with those who support and challenge you. Through networking or partnerships, community becomes an invaluable asset to propel your business forward.

Reflection on Passing Down Knowledge

As I took on more ventures, I realized the knowledge I gained wasn't just for me—it was meant to be shared. My stamp-dealing days taught me integrity, trust, and resilience—lessons I've passed to my children, grandchildren, and now, you. Entrepreneurship isn't just about money; it's about creating something meaningful to share with future generations.

Action Steps for New Entrepreneurs

- **Build Relationships Based on Trust**: Whether you're just starting or scaling your business, focus on creating strong, trustworthy relationships. It will be the bed- rock of your success.
- **Don't Wait for Perfect Conditions**: Get started with what you have.
- **Defend Your Values**: Like I did when my stamps were stolen, never shy away from defending what's important to you. Your principles will define your reputation as an entrepreneur.

Think About This

- When have you relied on trust to close a deal or collaboration? Did it succeed or fail, and why?
- What creative strategies have you used to make the most of limited resources?

- How does the concept of starting small and building momentum apply to your current goals?

How Would This Apply to You?
- Focus on building trust as your foundation. List one way you can enhance trust with your team or clients this week.
- Identify a negotiation you're currently facing. How can you apply creative problem-solving to make it a win-win?
- Reflect on a skill or hobby you have that could turn into a profitable venture. What's your first step?

"Trust is the currency of
every successful deal.
Without it, no negotiation
will stand the test of time."

*- David Selley
Entrepreneur, Author*

#2 PERSONAL MAILING SERVICES
Vancouver, Canada 1955

Long before the internet connected us all, David spotted an untapped opportunity in communication. But this venture wasn't just about innovation—it revealed a hidden truth about timing, efficiency, and knowing when to pivot. What happened next would surprise even him.

When I arrived in Vancouver and had my job with the telephone company, I came up with the idea of a personalized mailing service that would work for people who were too busy or lazy to "send out cards" In order to get a business license I needed an office so rented one cheap room in a run down part of town just to comply with the regulations. I only went into it once and then operated my new home based business from my rooming house room. To start this little business and with no real experience whatsoever and a high level of ignorance I proceeded to negotiate with some of the large greeting card companies and became a home-based dealer that was unheard of in those days of traditional retailing. This permitted me to get the sample books of greetings cards of all types at no cost whatsoever. I would make appointments with people; show them the sample books from which they would select the various cards to be mailed out on the customers predetermined schedule. This little business was a total failure for many reasons mainly because of poor planning and marketing skills but, today there is a flourishing networking business called "Send out Cards" and one of my friends Gwen Field in Hollywood is one of their top agents.

What I learned

I learned the critical importance of market research and understanding customer needs. I also discovered how to work with attorneys for the best value and gained insights into customer cost and profit margins (C.P.C.).

My biggest lesson was that success in business depends on understanding the market and effectively planning your approach. It's also a great reminder that many of the ideas I had early on were just ahead of their time, showing how technology and better marketing could have made this concept thrive today.

Takeaways from My Personalized Mailing Service in 1955

When I started my personalized mailing service in Vancouver, I was full of enthusiasm but lacked the knowledge that would have made it successful. The concept itself wasn't flawed—it was just ahead of its time. Here's what I learned from this failed venture:

Understand the Market Before You Launch

One key lesson I learned from this business was the importance of understanding your market. I jumped into the mailing service without considering whether there was enough demand or if people were willing to pay for the convenience. As an entrepreneur, you must do your homework. Market research is crucial—ensure there is demand for your product or service before investing time and money.

Planning is Everything

While enthusiasm can drive you to start a business, planning is what will help you sustain it. My lack of planning and marketing skills meant the business never gained traction. Nowadays, with all the resources available, there's no excuse for skipping the planning phase. Take time to outline your strategy, marketing approach, and target audience before diving in.

Timing Matters

Looking back, I realized my idea was ahead of its time. The concept of sending out cards for busy people, which seemed too niche back then, is now a thriving business model through companies like "Send Out Cards." Sometimes, you might have a brilliant idea, but the timing just isn't right. Learn to recognize when your idea needs to adapt to current trends and technology.

Practical Advice for Modern Entrepreneurs

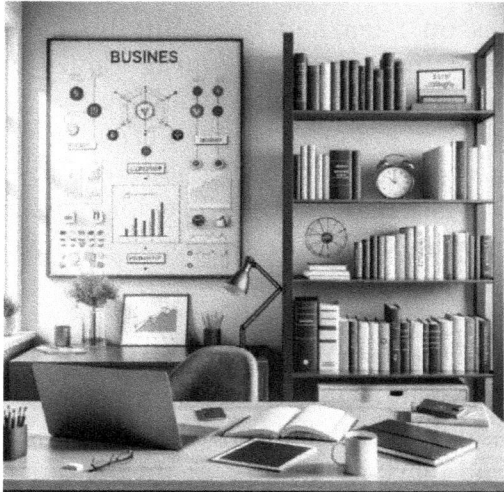

Research First, Act Second: Before launching any venture, make sure you fully understand your market, your customers, and your competition. Don't skip this step—it can save you from a failed venture.

Plan Your Path: A good idea needs a solid plan to back it up. Develop a clear strategy for how you will reach your customers and grow your business.

Historical and Cultural Context

In 1955, the idea of a home-based business was virtually unheard of. The retail industry was dominated by physical stores, and my attempt to operate from a rooming house was unconventional at best. Today, with the rise of online businesses and remote work, home-based ventures are the norm. My experience reflects how much the entrepreneurial landscape has evolved, offering more flexibility for modern businesses.

Inspiring Words

"The way to get started is to quit talking and begin doing."— *Walt Disney*

I learned that talking about your ideas is one thing but executing them well is another. Sometimes you need to get moving, but always back it up with solid planning and research.

Tie-In to Modern Entrepreneurial Challenges

Many entrepreneurs today struggle with the same challenge I faced—launching a product without enough research or planning. The key difference now is that we have access to countless tools for market analysis, business planning, and customer engagement. The lesson here is that no matter how exciting an idea might be, you have to ensure it's aligned with current demand and trends.

Community Building Tips

Even though this venture didn't succeed, it taught me the value of building connections with others. My interactions with greeting card companies gave me a foot in the door. For modern entrepreneurs, don't underestimate the importance of networking and forming partnerships, even in your early stages. Your network can often open doors to new opportunities or improvements for your business.

Reflection on Passing Down Knowledge

This venture reinforced the idea that failure is not the end—it's a steppingstone to future success. By passing on what I learned from this experience, I hope to show that even when a business doesn't work out, the lessons you gain are invaluable. Every failure is an opportunity to reflect, refine, and move forward.

Action Steps for New Entrepreneurs

- **Do Your Market Research**: Before you start any business, take the time to deeply understand your market and your potential customers.
- **Don't Skip the Planning Phase**: Enthusiasm is great, but it won't sustain a business on its own. Plan your strategy, map out your goals, and develop a marketing approach.
- **Adapt to the Times**: Sometimes, your idea may be ahead of its time. Keep an eye on technology and market trends, and don't be afraid to pivot if needed.

Think About This
- How do you recognize opportunities in the market that others might overlook?
- What systems do you have in place to ensure efficiency and scalability in your work?
- When have you learned from failing forward? How did that lesson shape your future decisions?

How Would This Apply to You?
- Analyze one recurring task in your business or life. How can you make it more efficient or delegate it?
- Consider a time when you missed an opportunity. What steps can you take now to ensure you don't miss the next one?
- Think about how you can innovate within your current industry. What's one small, unique service you can add to stand out?

#3 Lost & Found 1963

It seemed like the perfect idea: a service to solve one of life's most frustrating problems. But the path to success was anything but smooth. This venture taught David a lesson he never expected—one that would change how he approached every business decision that followed.

The Lost & Found idea was born in 1964 when I came up with a concept for a local, regional, national, and international recovery service. The idea was simple: lost or stolen personal property could be returned to its rightful owner by using a registration or serial number affixed to each item. Keep in mind, computer technology was still in its infancy at the time. I knew I needed a working model to make this a viable business, so I decided to test the idea in a specific market.

After noticing how often people posted about lost pets in the local newspaper, I decided that the strong emotional attachment people have to their pets made this the perfect test case. I had my friend Ted Poyser, a talented designer, create the Lost & Found logo. Ted designed two arrows circling the words "LOST AND FOUND" in a modern "euro style." Armed with a professional logo, I began developing my merchandising strategy.

I created anodized aluminum counter signs featuring a sample dog tag and explanatory graphics, along with a registration card. I visited pet stores, explaining the service and leaving the materials for customers to register their pets. This approach worked, and registrations started coming in. However, technology back then wasn't as advanced as today—there were no cell phones, answering machines, or call forwarding. Operating on a tight budget, I opted to have the calls come directly to my home, where I could personally take them and explain the service.

While working on this venture, I was also selling Smith Corona typewriters door-to-door in downtown Los Angeles. During one of my sales demos, I met a CPA who took an interest in my Lost & Found concept. He offered to introduce me to some of his high-level contacts in exchange for a share of the business. He also suggested registering the Lost & Found name as a trademark, which led to my first experience with attorneys. The trademark was successfully registered (872.332), and I was eager to take the next step.

Following my CPA friend's advice, I signed documents forming a Bermuda-based trust to manage the business's anticipated revenue, as there were supposed tax advantages. Unfortunately, I didn't read the fine print closely and ended up signing away 97% of my beneficial interest in the project. This was a major learning moment for me.

Despite this setback, the Lost & Found project continued to gain traction. I even met with executives at Samsonite, who showed interest in using the service to protect their luggage, and several major banks in San Francisco, who considered using the registration system to attract new customers. Unfortunately, the banking regulations at the time prevented the project from moving forward, and a similar lack of cooperation from the insurance industry led to the project being shelved.

At the end of the day, it was another great idea that didn't pan out due to unforeseen challenges.

What I Learned

I learned about basic marketing and negotiation skills, as well as the complexities of trademark, patent, copyright, and service mark registration.

My biggest lesson was that you must develop the skills

to check and fully understand everything you sign. Never rely solely on others, no matter how qualified they seem. Always have a qualified attorney reviewing any legal documents to protect your interests.

Key Takeaways from
My Lost & Found Venture in 1963

The Lost & Found service was an innovative idea—way ahead of its time in many ways. Although it didn't succeed as I had hoped, it provided me with a wealth of lessons, both in business and in navigating legal complexities. Here are the key takeaways from this venture:

Innovative Thinking Can Be Your Edge

The idea of using serial numbers to return lost items was an early example of thinking ahead of the curve. At a time when technology was barely in its infancy, I created a concept that would later become standard in various industries—from luggage recovery to pet ID tags. As an entrepreneur, your ability to see where trends may be heading is one of your greatest assets. Even if the timing isn't perfect, don't shy away from pushing forward with innovative ideas.

Legal Literacy is a Must

One of the most painful lessons I learned was the importance of thoroughly understanding legal agreements. The Bermuda-based trust deal looked good on paper, but I failed to fully grasp the implications of signing away 97% of my interest in the project. Always—always—read the fine print. More importantly, have a qualified attorney review any major documents, no matter how experienced or trusted your business partners may seem. This is a lesson worth repeating: protect your interests before committing yourself to anything legally binding.

Networking Can Open Doors (But Beware of Pitfalls)

My connection with the CPA opened some exciting possibilities, including meetings with Samsonite executives and major banks. However, I learned that not every door leads to success. Some of these opportunities were stalled by regulations or lack of cooperation from other industries. While networking is vital for getting ahead, it's equally important to recognize that not every lead will materialize into a winning partnership.

Practical Advice for Modern Entrepreneurs

Be Innovative but Stay Grounded: Don't be afraid to bring forward new ideas, even if they seem ahead of the times. However, ensure that your concept has a realistic plan and the right support in place for execution.

Master Legal Basics: Having legal knowledge is no longer optional. Learn the basics of contracts, trademarks, and patents, and always involve an attorney when making important decisions.

Historical and Cultural Context

In 1963, businesses operated in a much less connected world. There were no cell phones, no email, and no internet to instantly promote ideas or streamline services. In this context, my idea for Lost & Found was quite ambitious. The concept of creating a global registration system for lost property was futuristic for its time, and it took on challenges that only later became easier to manage with technological advancements.

Words of Wisdom

"Don't be afraid to give up the good to go for the great."
-John D. Rockefeller

This resonates deeply with the Lost & Found story. Sometimes, good ideas don't fully take off, but the experience gained in pursuit of greatness is what truly counts.

Tie-In to Modern Entrepreneurial Challenges

Many modern entrepreneurs face the same hurdles I encountered — great ideas that are stymied by regulations, technological limitations, or insufficient resources. In today's landscape, while technology is more advanced, the challenge of pushing an innovative idea through the clutter remains the same. The lesson here is resilience and adaptability. If your first idea doesn't work, keep refining it until it does—or pivot to something more viable for the time.

Community Building Tips

Building trust and goodwill is essential in any entrepreneurial venture. Even though my Lost & Found idea didn't reach full fruition, I was able to connect with influential business figures and companies. For any entrepreneur, fostering relationships and building a community around your idea—be it through networking or partnerships—will help you scale your business or pivot when needed.

Reflection on Passing Down Knowledge

One of the lasting lessons from the Lost & Found experience is the importance of passing down what you've learned—whether through successes or failures. The insights I gained about negotiation, legal literacy, and adapting to market needs are ones I now share with younger entrepreneurs. My missteps in the legal aspects of this venture are an important reminder to always protect your hard work and ideas. Passing these lessons on is part of creating a lasting entrepreneurial legacy.

Action Steps for New Entrepreneurs

- **Protect Your Intellectual Property**: Before launching a business idea, ensure that your name, logo, and any unique features are protected with trademarks or patents.

- **Build a Strong Legal Foundation**: Learn to read and understand contracts -- always have a trusted legal advisor review any deals before signing.

- **Network With Purpose**: Make connections but also recognize that not every opportunity will pan out. Be selective in who you partner with, and focus on building long-term, meaningful relationships.

Think About This
- Have you ever had an idea that seemed too risky to pursue? What made you hesitate?
- How do you evaluate the potential legal or logistical challenges of a new venture?
- What personal values guide your decision-making when faced with ethical dilemmas in business?

How Would This Apply to You?
- Assess one of your current ideas for risks and rewards. How can you mitigate the risks to make it more feasible?
- Write down a checklist of criteria to evaluate the practicality of your next business idea.
- Think about how you can align your next venture with both profitability and your personal values.

#4 Home Service Company

It started as a simple idea:
offering everyday services that everyone needed. But
what began as a straightforward plan quickly turned
into a masterclass in managing risks, clarifying
communication, and learning when to walk away. What
went wrong—and what valuable lessons came from it?

As the name suggests, the Home Service Company provided basic handyman services to homeowners, but on a contractual basis. After losing my job and needing to provide for my family, I had to think quickly. I became an apprentice of sorts to a friend who owned a carpet cleaning company. My goal wasn't to compete with him but to offer carpet cleaning as one of many services. After some research, I found niche areas of home maintenance that were underserved, such as window screen repairs and minor repairs for seniors who couldn't do it themselves. In essence, I became a central point for many services, and if I couldn't do a job myself, I would subcontract it out and take an override commission.

I advertised in six categories in the Yellow Pages, and soon the phone wouldn't stop ringing. I spent much of my time giving estimates and managing public relations. Before long, I had a steady clientele and focused on profitable services like window washing, carpet cleaning, and yard maintenance.

One of the most memorable stories from this time involved an elderly widow, Mrs. Sheffield, who needed regular yard work. When I visited her home to give an estimate, I noticed that her late husband had left behind a complete lapidary workshop. Intrigued by the craft of polishing stones, I offered a two-year contract for services in exchange for the entire workshop, which was a fair deal for both of us.

However, things took a wrong turn. I assigned the yard work to one of my trusted employees. A few days later, I received a frantic call from Mrs. Sheffield, upset about the work done. My worker had "trimmed" her 75-foot row of blooming rose bushes by two feet, destroying all the roses in full bloom. It was a disaster I couldn't fix, and she immediately canceled the contract. There went my opportunity to explore lapidary, a skill I still have on my bucket list.

What I Learned

Make sure that when you assign a task to someone, they have a complete and accurate understanding of the job by asking them to explain what you've asked them to do. It sounds simple, but the same word can mean entirely different things to different people, so it's critical to be VERY specific with instructions. Don't take anything for granted and remember that things aren't always what they seem.

Also, never forget the old adage: "Don't bite off more than you can chew." It's not just a saying; it's a survival tactic in business. If you take on too much without fully understanding the risks, it can come back to bite you.

My biggest lesson was that clear communication is essential, and you can't assume others will interpret instructions the same way you do. Confirming understanding before moving forward is vital, especially when the outcome could have significant consequences for your business.

The Tree Story

Another advertisement in the Yellow Pages was for tree trimming, which led to many calls. One memorable case involved a man who claimed his 70–80-foot tree was sick. Not having any expertise in tree care, I inspected the tree as best as I could and told him I needed to do some "botanical research." I went to the library, learned about the poplar tree, and discovered that the problem was simply a lack of water. A broken valve had prevented water from reaching the roots. After fixing the irrigation, the tree revived, and the owner was overjoyed, even crediting me as an expert.

What I Learned

I learned the value of research, even when entering unfamiliar territory. Admitting that you don't know something but are willing to learn can go a long way with clients. Taking the time to understand the situation thoroughly allowed me to solve the problem effectively and gain the client's trust.

Admitting when you don't know something but are willing to learn can go a long way with clients. Taking the time to do proper research allows you to solve problems effectively and builds trust. The most valuable lesson here is that clients appreciate honesty and the effort to learn—even when you're out of your comfort zone.

The Power of Research

When I encountered a sick tree that was well beyond my knowledge, I could have walked away or guessed at the solution. Instead, did research at the library, and discovered it was a simple lack of water due to a broken valve. After solving the problem, the client saw me as an expert, even though I had learned on the job.

My biggest lesson was that clients appreciate honesty and effort, and sometimes, solving a problem requires going back to the basics—like water for a tree.

The Wallpaper Removal Incident

Another service I offered was wallpaper removal, even though I had never done it before. I accepted a job from an acquaintance to remove foil-backed cork wallpaper. After doing some research, I acquired the necessary tools and equipment, including a steamer, but quickly realized this method wouldn't work due to the foil backing. The homeowner noticed my inexperience but appreciated my honesty, and we ended up working together to remove the wallpaper. Although it was a tough job, I was paid for the work and learned valuable lessons along the way.

Learning Alongside the Client

I took on a wallpaper removal job that I had never done before, using tools and techniques I hadn't yet mastered. When I realized my method wasn't working, I admitted my inexperience to the homeowner, and we ended up working together to get the job done. Even though it wasn't perfect, the client appreciated my honesty, and I was still paid for the work.

What I Learned

In both cases, I learned that it's okay to admit when you don't know something, but it's important to be willing to learn. I also realized that with enough research, you can solve most problems, even ones outside your expertise.

It's okay to admit when you're in over your head, but you must be willing to learn and adapt. Clients respect honesty, especially when they see you making an effort. In business, sometimes the best solution is collaboration, and learning alongside your client can still lead to positive outcomes.

My biggest lesson was that honesty goes a long way in business and being upfront with clients when you're learning something new can often earn their respect.

The Sprinkler System Idea

Lastly, I developed a portable automated sprinkler system to maintain lawns for vacant homes or vacationing homeowners. The system worked fine in most cases, but disaster struck when I installed it on a hillside property. Due to a malfunction, the sprinkler ran all night, nearly causing a retaining wall to collapse. Thankfully, the damage wasn't severe, but it was a close call. I had neglected to get insurance, which was a foolish decision.

Managing Risks

My idea for a portable automated sprinkler system was a creative solution for maintaining lawns, but when it malfunctioned on a hillside property and nearly caused significant damage, I realized I had overlooked key risks. The lack of insurance was a costly oversight that could have ended much worse.

What I Learned

I learned that even a good idea can fail if the risks aren't properly managed. While the need for the service was real, I underestimated the potential hazards.

Even the best ideas can fail if the risks aren't properly managed. Entrepreneurship involves risk-taking, but it's crucial to proceed cautiously, especially when dealing with situations that could have serious consequences. Always have safeguards in place, such as insurance, to protect yourself from unforeseen disasters.

My biggest lesson was that taking risks is part of entrepreneurship, but you must be prepared for unforeseen consequences. Sometimes, it's better to proceed cautiously and have safeguards in place.

Key Takeaways from My Home Service Company Venture

Running the Home Service Company taught me valuable lessons about communication, honesty, and taking calculated risks. Each service I provided revealed new insights, and I learned to adapt quickly in order to keep the business running smoothly. Here are the overarching lessons from this venture:

Clear Communication is the Cornerstone of Success

One of the most important lessons I learned was the critical importance of clear communication. My experience with Mrs. Sheffield's roses was a painful reminder of this. When you delegate tasks, always ask your team to explain back to you what they heard to avoid any misunderstandings.

Don't Overextend Yourself

Running multiple services under one roof required me to manage many different tasks and clients. This taught me that while expanding your service offerings can be profitable, it's crucial not to overextend yourself. You need the resources and time to manage each service effectively.

Honesty and Effort Win Client Trust

Across the services I offered, honesty became a cornerstone of my approach. Clients valued my willingness to admit when I didn't know something and to learn. Building trust through honesty makes clients more understanding of the learning process and more likely to work with you.

Practical Advice for Modern Entrepreneurs

Communicate Clearly and Verify Understanding: Don't assume people will understand instructions the way you do. Always verify.

Be Willing to Learn: In any industry, there will be times when you don't know something. Take those opportunities to learn and build trust with clients.

Manage Risks: When dealing with services that carry risks, always be prepared for the worst. Get insurance and have contingency plans in place.

Action Steps for New Entrepreneurs

- **Confirm Understanding**: Make sure your team or subcontractors know exactly what you expect by having them explain the task back to you.

- **Admit When You Don't Know Something**: Clients respect honesty. If you don't have the answer, be willing to learn and figure it out.

- **Protect Your Business**: Don't take unnecessary risks. Always ensure you have insurance or contingency plans for high-risk services.

Think About This

• Have you ever taken on too many responsibilities at once? How did it affect your outcomes?
• When have unclear expectations or miscommunications caused a challenge in your business or personal life?
• How do you evaluate the risks involved before committing to a new venture or project?

How Would This Apply to You?

• Focus on creating clear, written expectations for any new project or partnership.

• Assess the current risks in one of your ongoing projects—what's your plan to mitigate them?

• Think about delegating tasks in your business to ensure you're not stretched too thin.

"Clear communication isn't just good practice—it's the foundation of trust and success."

- David Selley
Entrepreneur, Author

#5 Sure Safe Auto Device

An innovative idea with massive potential—
until it wasn't. This venture highlighted the importance of
safety, thorough testing, and understanding hidden risks.
Could you have anticipated the pitfalls David faced?
Only one way to find out.

Having an inventive mind, I was introduced to a young man through a neighbor who had developed a product designed to prevent car thefts. Fascinated by the potential, I immediately expressed interest in exploring this opportunity to make some big money—or so I thought. The device was a combination of electronics and mechanics. In simple terms, it worked by interrupting the ignition process unless a safety button, known only to the driver, was switched off.

When the driver left the vehicle, they would leave the switch on so that a thief, unaware of the safety feature, could attempt to start the car either by jump-starting it or using a key. The device would then interrupt the ignition firing process within 10 to 15 seconds, causing the car to stall and rendering it inoperable.

It sounded great on paper, but during field tests, we encountered several issues. In some cases, we fried ignition wiring systems, and there were a few near-fatal accidents as a result of the product malfunctioning. These incidents made it clear that further development and large-scale testing would be prohibitively expensive, not to mention the serious insurance risks involved.

While testing the product with friends and even some skeptics, we ran into many problems. People often forgot to turn the hidden safety switch on or off, leading to dangerous situations, such as stalling on freeways or busy streets. After numerous consultations with attorneys, we ultimately decided to abandon the project.

What I Learned

I learned that while having a good idea is valuable, it's crucial to assess the risks and costs of bringing that idea to life. Sometimes, the potential liabilities far outweigh the rewards.

My biggest lesson was that good ideas are plentiful, but taking them to market requires more than just enthusiasm. You need to understand the broader implications, including safety, cost, and the competition you might face from established industries like the auto industry. Many of today's cars come with built-in anti-theft systems—an example of how larger companies respond to market demand, often with more resources and infrastructure in place.

Key Takeaways from the Sure Safe Auto Device

The Sure Safe Auto Device was a promising idea that ultimately failed due to significant safety concerns and the costs associated with bringing it to market. This experience taught me some hard but essential lessons about product development, risk management, and the importance of understanding both the market and the industry you're trying to enter. Here are the key takeaways from this venture:

Great Ideas Are Only the Beginning

Having a great idea is exciting, but it's just the first step. When we developed the Sure Safe Auto Device, it looked excellent on paper, and the potential was huge. However, as we began testing, we quickly realized that the execution of the idea was flawed. Malfunctions and safety risks caused us to halt the project. This taught me that while great ideas are valuable, they are only the foundation—bringing them to life requires extensive testing, refinement, and sometimes, the realization that they may not be viable.

Assess Risk Before Moving Forward

One of the biggest lessons I learned from this venture was the importance of assessing risk early on. Field tests revealed significant safety issues, including dangerous malfunctions that could have led to serious accidents. These risks, combined with the high cost of further testing and development, outweighed the potential rewards. As an entrepreneur, it's crucial to conduct a risk assessment before fully committing to a new project. Sometimes, the risks—whether financial, legal, or safety-related—are too great to proceed.

The Cost of Competing with Industry Giants

The auto industry is a highly competitive space, with established companies investing millions into research and development. Our product was eventually abandoned because we didn't have the resources to compete with major automakers who were already developing integrated anti-theft systems. This experience taught me that when you're entering a market dominated by giants, you need to understand the challenges ahead. It's essential to know when to pivot or walk away when the competition is too steep and the costs are too high.

Practical Advice for Modern Entrepreneurs

Develop and Test Your Ideas Thoroughly: A good idea on paper may not translate into a good product in reality. Test extensively and refine your product before moving forward.

Conduct Risk Assessments Early: Identify all potential risks—financial, legal, and safety-related — before moving a project into full-scale development.

Know Your Competition: Entering a market with established players can be daunting. Assess whether you have the resources to compete or if it's better to pivot.

Lessons from the Field: The Value of Safety

While testing the Sure Safe Auto Device, we encountered significant issues, from fried ignition systems to near-fatal malfunctions. This experience reminded me that safety has to be a top priority in product development. No matter how promising an idea might seem, if it poses a danger to users, it's not worth pursuing. It's easy to get caught up in the excitement of a new venture, but it's vital to take a step back and think critically about the risks involved.

Product safety should never be compromised. Whether you're working on a physical product or a digital service, ensuring the safety and well-being of your users is paramount. Sometimes this means walking away from a promising idea if it poses too much risk.

Insights from the Sure Safe Device Failure:

Managing Legal and Insurance Issues

One of the critical lessons from this venture was the role of legal and insurance concerns. The product posed too many potential liabilities, and further development would have required significant investment in legal protections and insurance coverage. These costs, along with the risks, made the project unsustainable.

In any business, understanding the legal landscape is crucial. Products that could pose risks need to be protected by solid legal frameworks, including insurance and liability agreements. Always consult with legal professionals early in the development process to avoid costly mistakes down the road.

Takeaways from Abandoning the Project:

Knowing When to Walk Away

At some point, every entrepreneur will face a project that doesn't go as planned. For me, the Sure Safe Auto Device was that project. After months of work, consultations with attorneys, and field tests, we decided to abandon the product. While disappointing, this decision was necessary. Knowing when to walk away can be as important as knowing when to pursue a great idea.

Sometimes, the best decision you can make is to cut your losses and move on. Not every idea will be a success, and it's vital to recognize when the risks and costs outweigh the potential rewards. This ability to pivot is essential in business.

Practical Advice for Modern Entrepreneurs

Prioritize Safety: No matter how great your idea seems, it must prioritize user safety. If safety is compromised, reconsider the project.

Consult Legal Experts: Always involve attorneys and insurance experts when developing a product with potential risks.

Know When to Walk Away: There's no shame in abandoning a project when it's no longer viable. Be willing to pivot and focus on new opportunities.

Action Steps for New Entrepreneurs

- **Assess Risks Thoroughly:** Before moving forward with any product, especially one that could impact safety, take the time to fully assess all potential risks. Ask yourself, "What's the worst that could happen?" and be prepared to mitigate those risks.

- **Invest in Testing and Development:** A good idea on paper needs to be thoroughly tested in real-world conditions. Make sure you budget for the development costs, including multiple rounds of testing, to ensure the product works as intended without introducing new problems.

- **Get Legal and Insurance Protections Early:** Before moving too far into development, make sure you consult with legal professionals about liability, patents, and insurance. If your product has the potential to cause harm, it's crucial to have legal and financial protections in place.

- **Understand Your Market:** Good ideas are everywhere, but larger companies often have the resources to bring similar products to market faster and more efficiently. Research your competition and determine whether your product can survive against established players.

- **Know When to Walk Away:** Sometimes, even the best ideas don't make it to market. Be prepared to abandon a project if the risks outweigh the potential rewards. Knowing when to cut your losses is as important as knowing when to press forward.

Think About This

- Have you ever been excited about an idea without fully exploring the risks? What happened?
- How do you ensure a product or service meets both customer expectations and safety standards?
- What's your process for testing new ideas before launching them?

How Would This Apply to You?

- Before pursuing a new idea, create a checklist of potential risks and ways to mitigate them.
- Identify one area in your current business where customer safety or satisfaction could be improved.
- Think about how you can better validate new ideas before committing significant resources to them

> "An idea is only as strong as the effort you put into making it safe, reliable, and valuable."
>
> *- David Selley*
> *Entrepreneur, Author*

#6 Sonja's Food & Gifts

*A gourmet shop seemed like a dream business—
until the realities of trends, competition, and market
demands came into play. This venture revealed the
delicate balance between passion and practicality in
building a lasting enterprise.*

Before, during, and after my termination from my last major corporate job, we were looking at other income alternatives. I saw a seminar about how to buy a business for nothing down, which reminded me of my stamp-buying days as a kid. I enrolled in the seminar, paid the $1,000 fee for two days of training at a prominent hotel in Los Angeles, and learned the essential skills to buy a business without an upfront payment.

We contacted a commercial real estate broker to outline our requirements. Although he was skeptical, I knew something he didn't—how to buy a business for nothing down. About a week later, he called about a unique situation: a failing wine, lunch, and gourmet food business was for sale, with personal problems leading the owners to close it for a while. We set up an appointment to meet.

The business was a mess. It had moved to a smaller location, and when we arrived, we were greeted by the rancid smell of rotten meats and cheeses because the electricity had been off for weeks. However, the place was filled with valuable items, including hundreds of bottles of wine, a rare Gaggia espresso machine worth thousands of dollars, and expensive cutlery and gifts. Despite the mess, the inventory and equipment totaled approximately $30,000 in value.

After a long discussion at home, my wife and I decided to make a list of possibilities. We knew the current circumstances, but we saw potential and created a plan. We offered $500 down and a $6,000 purchase price, along with conditions such as a UCC1 Filing, immediate occupancy, and a 90-day escrow. The offer was accepted immediately.

We liquidated the inventory to pay off the purchase price and fund operations. We then transformed the shop into **Sonja's Food & Gifts**, an English tea shop with a traditional English look, featuring Thomas Kincaid paintings, blue-and-white checkerboard tablecloths, and Blue Willow china. My wife's exceptional culinary skills shaped the menu, and we offered large, memorable sandwiches named after mountains. We followed advice from a friend: "Give them something they will never forget," leading to higher profit margins and a unique dining experience.

After a soft opening to iron out any operational kinks, word spread quickly. On our grand opening day, the shop was packed, with lines out the door. It was an instant success, and over the next few months, we developed a steady rhythm to handle the increasing business.

One month in, I received a call from Sonja about a Small Business Administration (SBA) investigator who had come by threatening to shut us down due to a $250,000 loan default by the previous owners. Thankfully, I had included specific language in our purchase offer and escrow instructions, which protected us from this liability. While the SBA placed a lien on the escrow, we were in the clear.

Our daughter helped at the shop after school, and one day I decided to play a prank. I hid five $100 bills under dirty plates, and when she found them while cleaning, she was thrilled. It was a fun family moment.

A particularly humorous incident occurred when a customer ordered iced tea. Growing up in England, where iced tea wasn't common, I had no idea how to make it. I brewed hot tea, added ice, and mixed it in the milkshake machine—unbeknownst to me, there was still some leftover vanilla ice cream in the tumbler. To my surprise, the customer loved it!

Eventually, a German couple bought the shop, and we made a handsome profit. Unfortunately, they turned it into a deli, and it went out of business a year later.

What I Learned

The bottom line was that we spotted a trend and recognized the need for a high-end boutique in our area, catering to affluent customers who valued quality and were willing to pay for it. By working hard and being persistent, we created our market and delivered a top-tier product with a memorable dining experience.

My biggest lesson was that if you provide something unique and of high quality, customers will come—and they'll remember the experience long after they've forgotten the price.

Key Takeaways
from Sonja's Food & Gifts

Running Sonja's Food & Gifts wasn't just a business—it was a labor of love, a family affair, and an exercise in seeing opportunity where others saw obstacles. This venture taught me invaluable lessons about recognizing market trends, delivering quality, and creating an experience that customers would never forget.

Spotting Trends and Seizing Opportunity
in the Midst of Chaos

When we first saw the business, it was in terrible shape—rotten inventory, a bad reputation, and significant financial troubles. Most people would have walked away. But we saw potential. The key was spotting the trend of high-end, boutique food experiences and recognizing that the affluent local market would respond positively to an English tea shop offering something different. The lesson here is that opportunities often come disguised as problems. The key to success is seeing what others overlook and having the confidence to act.

Turning Challenges into Opportunity:
Creative Solutions

We didn't have much capital to work with, but we turned the problem into a solution. Liquidating the existing inventory helped fund the transition into Sonja's Food & Gifts, and we were able to use the valuable equipment and wine stock to pay off the purchase price. This taught me that creative problem-solving and resourcefulness are crucial in business—especially when working with limited resources.

Give Them Something They'll Never Forget

One of the most important things I learned from this venture is that success doesn't just come from offering a good product—it comes from creating a memorable experience. Everything about Sonja's Food & Gifts was designed to be unique, from the Blue Willow China to the oversized sandwiches named after mountains. My wife's culinary skills and the traditional English atmosphere were key to this, but the idea of leaving a lasting impression on customers is what made it thrive. In business, always aim to give people more than what they expect.

Always Be Prepared for the Unexpected

One month into running the shop, we were blindsided by an SBA investigator threatening to shut us down due to the previous owner's $250,000 loan default. Fortunately, my careful attention to legal details in the escrow agreement protected us. This was a critical reminder of the importance of anticipating potential challenges and ensuring your agreements protect you from past liabilities.

Practical Advice for Modern Entrepreneurs

Spot Opportunities in Unlikely Places: Don't shy away from a business that looks like it's failing. With the right vision and strategy, you can turn it around.

Solve Problems Creatively: When working with limited resources, think outside the box. Turn what seems like a disadvantage into an opportunity.

Create an Unforgettable Customer Experience: In today's crowded market, it's not enough to offer a good product—make sure the experience is something people will remember.

Protect Yourself Legally: Always ensure your contracts and agreements protect you from any hidden liabilities or issues from previous ownership.

Action Steps for New Entrepreneurs

- Identify Hidden Value: Sometimes, what appears to be a failing business has assets or untapped potential that can be leveraged for success. Learn to see the opportunities others might miss.

- Invest in Customer Experience: Go beyond delivering a product. Think about the full experience your customers will have and how you can make it unique and memorable.

- Prepare for the Unexpected: Be thorough in your legal agreements, and always ensure you're protected from past liabilities or debts.

Think About This

- When have you pursued a passion project? Did it meet your expectations or teach you unexpected lessons?
- How do you gauge whether a trend is worth investing in, or if it's fleeting?
- What steps can you take to deliver a unique and memorable experience to your customers?

How Would This Apply to You?

- Think about how you can improve the customer experience in your current work—what makes it stand out?
- Identify one trend in your industry that could offer a new opportunity or competitive edge.
- Reflect on how to balance your personal passion with practical considerations in your business decisions.

> "Passion fuels the dream,
> but practicality keeps it alive."
>
> *- David Selley*
> *Entrepreneur, Author*

#7 The Gourmet Chalet

*Purchasing a seasonal gourmet deli in
Tahoe City seemed like a dream—charming location,
loyal customers, and a thriving tourist season. However, it
quickly revealed harsh lessons about emotional decisions
and the challenges of seasonal businesses.*

Let me take you back to the Gourmet Chalet story and prove once again how emotions can outpace logic. It was late September when I was driving with a friend of mine in his motor home over Donner Pass, heading toward Reno. We saw a sign for Tahoe City, just 14 miles away. The fall foliage was breathtaking, with shades of orange, crimson, and brown covering the mountains. Caught up in the beauty of the moment, we decided to take a detour and check it out.

As we wound through the 14 miles along the Truckee River, we were awestruck by the panoramic views. The crisp, fresh air and the beautiful blue sky were an invitation to explore. As we drove into Tahoe City, I noticed a two-story building that stood out from the rest—a uniquely Tyrolean-themed store called the Gourmet Chalet. Its large hand-carved wooden sign caught my eye, and I couldn't resist stopping to take a look.

The inside was just as impressive: a 4,000-square-foot full-service deli with a 120-pod wine cellar, 40 to 50 types of beer, a complete array of gourmet packaged goods, meats, cheeses, and high-end champagnes. The place also had a 700-square-foot space in the back, which would later become a small takeout pizza parlor. It came fully equipped with three cash registers, all the necessary deli equipment, and a security camera system.

What happened next is something you MUST NEVER, EVER, DO: I walked up to the owner and asked, "Is this place for sale?" He replied, "Could be." I then asked, "How much are you asking?" He said, "$286,000 plus inventory." Without thinking, I responded, "Are you open to terms?" In a matter of minutes, I made several fatal mistakes. Despite having learned not to let emotions cloud logic, I had fallen into the trap.

What followed was a two-year nightmare. The business turned out to be highly seasonal, thriving only during the winter ski season and summer tourist months. We moved from our home in Westlake Village, California, during a time of 17.5% interest rates and $2.57 per gallon gasoline prices. We were losing $2,000 a month, but we were committed to making it work.

To make matters worse, we faced several unexpected challenges. We were robbed at gunpoint in our first week. The snow didn't arrive until late February, and the liquor license we needed was delayed by several months. On top of that, two $3,400 cooler compressors failed during a record 93-degree heatwave. Our son Steven was also injured in a school bus accident, adding to the chaos.

Despite the hardships, there were some lighter moments worth mentioning. One day, a man with a bad attitude stormed into the store, demanding to know the price of a bottle of wine. After several exchanges, I politely asked him to leave my store, feeling that I didn't need his business. Another time, a logger couple from a convention ordered two of our largest pizzas. The man tripped over a dog leash on his way out, spilling the hot pizza onto his chest. We quickly diffused the situation by offering them a free meal and some wine, and they left without following through on their threats to sue.

What I Learned

This experience taught me the dangers of making emotional decisions in business. I learned that a seasonal business can be extremely challenging without the right preparation and research. Additionally, I learned how important it is to fully understand the financial and operational realities of a business before diving in.

Never make a rushed decision without weighing the risks. **"Don't bite off more than you can chew"** became my mantra in this situation—sometimes it's better to pause and assess rather than jump into a venture based on emotions alone.

My biggest lesson was that emotions can cloud judgment, and while optimism is important, thorough research and planning are essential to avoiding disaster.

Key Takeaways
from The Gourmet Chalet

The story of *The Gourmet Chalet* taught me critical lessons about the dangers of making hasty decisions driven by emotion, and the importance of thorough research and planning. This experience also highlighted the unique challenges of running a seasonal business and how unexpected events can test your resilience.

Emotion Can Cloud Judgment –
Always Do Your Du Diligence

I let my emotions get the better of me when I fell in love with the charm of the Gourmet Chalet and the beauty of Lake Tahoe. Without thinking it through, I initiated negotiations with the owner before understanding the true financial and operational realities of the business. This taught me that in entrepreneurship, you must separate your personal excitement from business decisions. Always back your instincts with thorough due diligence, research, and fact-based analysis before making a move.

Seasonal Businesses:
More Than Just Peak Times

The romantic idea of running a charming mountain business was shattered by the harsh reality of a highly seasonal business. A seasonal business may thrive for a few months of the year, but if the rest of the year is financially draining, it's incredibly difficult to stay afloat. Managing cash flow, predicting off-season revenue drops, and planning for cyclical demand should be at the top of the checklist for anyone entering a business like this. My failure to understand this up front led to significant losses. The lesson here? Know when the money will come in—and more importantly, when it won't.

Financial Buffers Are Critical

The unexpected challenges we faced—such as a delayed liquor license, broken cooler compressors, and even a robbery—could have sunk us if we hadn't had some financial reserves in place. The takeaway is simple but crucial: always plan for the worst-case scenario. Make sure your business has a financial buffer to handle unforeseen events, because in entrepreneurship, the unexpected can—and will—happen. Resilience and flexibility come from having a cushion that can absorb the blow of unexpected costs.

Never Underestimate the Power of Location and Timing

The location of the Gourmet Chalet played a double-edged role in our experience. Tahoe City was gorgeous and bustling during peak tourist seasons, but that same location became a ghost town in the off-season. A great location during one season can become a dead zone in another, so it's essential to factor in local economic cycles, customer traffic patterns, and how timing can affect business performance. This is a critical factor for any business relying on foot traffic.

Overcome Setbacks with Creativity and Resilience

Despite the many setbacks, I had to remain adaptable. When the logger tripped and spilled pizza all over himself, quick thinking, good customer service, and a free meal turned what could have been a disaster into a positive outcome. This event reinforced that, in business, flexibility and maintaining a positive relationship with customers can salvage difficult situations. Handling customer problems with grace and generosity is a lesson that applies to any entrepreneur.

Legal and Contractual Safeguards Are Essential

When the SBA showed up, I was incredibly thankful that I had included protections in the contract. Having the right legal language in place saved us from inheriting the financial mess left by the previous owners. The lesson? Always protect yourself legally, especially when taking over an existing business. Carefully review every contract and ensure you're shielded from the liabilities of the previous owners.

Practical Advice for Modern Entrepreneurs

Don't Let Passion Blind You: It's easy to get caught up in the excitement of a new venture, but it's crucial to take a step back and evaluate the opportunity logically. Emotions can lead to rushed decisions, but success comes from combining passion with sound judgment and thorough research.

Plan for Seasonal Variations: If you're entering a seasonal business, make sure you understand the cash flow implications of off-peak periods. Develop strategies to diversify income streams or manage costs during the slower months.

Always Have a Safety Net: Unexpected setbacks are part of running a business. Having a financial cushion in place allows you to weather storms, from broken equipment to market fluctuations.

Understand Your Market Dynamics: A perfect location in peak season can become a burden in the off-season. Research the area thoroughly to understand the ebb and flow of customer traffic. Timing, foot traffic, and local trends are key factors in deciding on a business location.

Focus on Customer Service: Even in tough times, great customer service can turn a problem into an opportunity. Handling mishaps with grace can build long-term loyalty and goodwill.

Action Steps for New Entrepreneurs

- **Do Your Research**: Always investigate a business's financials, market trends, and risks before committing. Don't let emotions drive your decisions.

- **Plan for Seasonality**: Understand cash flow during peak and off-peak seasons. Consider diversifying to generate income year-round.

- **Build a Financial Cushion**: Set aside reserves to handle unexpected costs, like equipment failures or delayed licensing.

- **Assess Location Carefully**: Analyze foot traffic and market dynamics for both busy and slow seasons before choosing a location.

- **Prioritize Customer Service**: Great customer service can turn problems into opportunities. Address issues swiftly to build loyalty.

- **Protect Yourself Legally**: Ensure contracts protect you from previous liabilities when buying an existing business. Always consult a lawyer.

Think About This:

- Are you making decisions based on emotions or careful analysis?

- Have you assessed the financial and operational demands of your business idea across all seasons?

- What contingency plans do you have if your primary revenue season underperforms?

- Do you fully understand the risks and challenges of your industry before committing?

How Would This Apply to You?

- Understand Your Market Cycles: If your business relies on seasonal revenue, explore ways to diversify your income streams during the off-season.

- Plan for the Worst: Always factor in the possibility of underwhelming performance during your best season.

- Separate Passion from Practicality: Loving a business idea is important, but ensure the numbers work before you dive in.

- Do Your Homework: Research is not just about the market—it's about understanding all aspects of the business, from operations to customer expectations.

> "Emotion may spark an idea,
> but only research and planning
> can build a lasting business."
>
> - David Selley
> Entrepreneur, Author

#8 The Tube Top Turnaround

In the ever-evolving world of fashion, staying ahead of trends is both an art and a science. David's venture into the tube top market was a bold move that tested his adaptability and resilience. The journey was filled with unexpected twists, offering invaluable lessons in innovation and market dynamics.

When it became obvious to me that The Gourmet Chalet was going downhill, I realized the powerful need to find something else that would help reverse or at least keep me financially stable. One day, I recalled one of the "nothing down" business deals I had been looking at, but the decision to move forward with The Gourmet Chalet had taken precedence.

While still in Thousand Oaks, CA I secured the services of several business brokers. They began telling me about various businesses that fit my purchase and control requirements. One particular referral was known as Mr. Brief (a one-size-fits-all men's brief). Before I get into the details, I want to emphasize that when a business is for sale, you must always dig deep to find out the real reasons *why* it is for sale. In most instances, you will get glowing reports about all the positive aspects of the business. Even when the reasons seem plausible, you are well-advised to do forensic-level background work to possibly uncover hidden issues. Hire a good attorney and accountant to do their due diligence, and make sure you include clauses in the contract to protect you in case of any details that were hidden or deliberately omitted.

In this case, some interesting things happened. This business, now closed and for sale, had national distribution in major department stores. The business carried $130,000 of debt on the books, a $30,000 inventory, a lease, and office equipment. The key benefit I saw was that they owned a specialty manufacturing process: a licensed and patented double-reverse stitching process performed on a European-made machine operated by a company in New England. I was fascinated by the process and decided to take a deeper look at why the business had closed. I made a tender offer to take control, including several "subject-to" clauses. Then I took a brief trip to the manufacturing plant in New England and to various department store headquarters to find out the facts.

In quick order, I discovered several key reasons for the closure. First, they had not paid for their production resources and had failed to deliver to their major accounts. Upon my return, the seller was anxious to move forward and even prepared a 27-page legal document absolving me of any liability if I bought the business. After a few meetings, however, the whole deal didn't pass the smell test. Almost instantly, I began to look beyond the current problems. My creative process kicked in, and I came up with an alternative. I decided not to buy the business but instead to take control of the manufacturing process. At the same time, I came up with the idea to jump on board with a new and popular teenage garment called the "tube top."

This garment was selling well in the women's market. It was literally a one-size-fits-all tube top that enhanced the female figure, was very simple to use, and was very fashionable at the time. I came up with the idea to develop a mail-order business featuring nine colors and fulfillment shipping. My reasoning was simple: the retail market had already been badly bruised by the previous owner's failures, and rebuilding confidence and trust would take a lot of time and money. Following up on negotiated contracts for manufacturing, I began to focus on fulfillment and shipping. Wanting to give back, I met with a performance-handicapped fulfillment center, which signed a contract to handle the fulfillment. The process was straightforward: customers selected one of the nine numbered colors, and the product was mailed directly to them.

With that agreement in place, I contracted with some major magazines and booked a series of ads in various teen magazines. With The Gourmet Chalet going down-hill financially, I began to see a glimmer of hope and dreamed of a mailbox full of thousands of orders. Guess what? That actually happened. But what happened next is a bit of a mindblower.

I went to the post office daily to pick up orders. Then we prepared mailing labels based on the color numbers selected by the customers. The labels were shipped to the fulfillment center in New England. Things went well for several weeks until one day, I got a call from a postmaster. He told me that if I didn't fix the problem quickly, my picture would be on the post office wall as a crook! He explained that many people had complained they had paid for the product but hadn't received their shipment.

Stunned, I tried contacting the fulfillment center, but no one answered. I called local contacts and discovered the director (my main contact) had arbitrarily closed for a month on vacation. Now I faced a major problem. Federal mail-order business laws are strict, and my unintentional violation of them put immense pressure on me to resolve the issue immediately.

By the time the fulfillment center reopened, it was too late. I hired several people to contact unhappy customers and assure them their orders were finally underway. We completed all the outstanding orders, but the damage was done. The problem exploded over those weeks, and the bad publicity quickly ended the opportunity.

What I Learned

Due Diligence is Essential: Never take a business's financial and operational claims at face value. Thorough investigation is key to understanding the true state of any business.

The Importance of Reliable Partnerships: The failure of the fulfillment center to deliver on their promises created a catastrophic issue. Choosing reliable partners and having contingency plans is crucial.

Adaptability is a Key Asset: The decision not to buy the business but instead pivot to a mail-order operation for tube tops demonstrated how thinking creatively can lead to new opportunities.

Legal and Operational Knowledge is Vital: My unintentional violation of federal mail-order laws was a harsh lesson in understanding and adhering to regulatory requirements.

Key Takeaways from the Tube Top Venture

Due Diligence is Non-Negotiable: When evaluating a business opportunity, dig deeper than surface-level information. Ask critical questions, investigate thoroughly, and involve professionals like attorneys and accountants to uncover hidden liabilities.

Reliability in Partnerships is Crucial: The collapse of the fulfillment center highlighted the importance of choosing reliable partners. Contingency plans should always be in place for key operational elements.

Creative Thinking Can Lead to New Opportunities: Pivoting from the failing Mr. Brief business to a mail-order tube top business showed the power of adaptability. Entrepreneurs must be willing to shift gears when the initial plan doesn't work out.

Understand the Legal Landscape: Unintended violations of federal mail-order laws were a costly lesson. Entrepreneurs must ensure they understand all applicable legal and regulatory requirements.

Practical Advice for Modern Entrepreneurs

Research Before You Leap: Always verify the background of businesses or partners before making decisions. Forensic-level due diligence can save you from future headaches.

Develop Backup Plans: Identify potential weak points in your operations and have alternative solutions ready to deploy if something goes wrong.

Focus on Customer Trust: Maintaining customer trust should always be a priority. Respond to issues quickly to preserve your reputation.

Stay Legal: Understand the laws governing your business operations. Hire experts if needed to navigate complex legal or regulatory landscapes.

Historical and Cultural Context

At the time of this venture, the retail and mail-order landscape operated without the advanced technologies we have today. Orders were handled manually, and communication relied heavily on phones and mail. In this environment, the tube top business required logistical coordination and trust, which became its Achilles' heel when the fulfillment center failed.

Words of Wisdom
"Opportunities don't happen. You create them." — Chris Grosser

This resonates with the tube top story. By recognizing the opportunity to pivot and adapt, I created a new venture despite the challenges. However, proper execution and follow-through are what ultimately sustain success.

Tie-In to Modern Entrepreneurial Challenges

Modern entrepreneurs face similar challenges: Unreliable partners, supply chain issues, and customer dissatisfaction. While technology has made many processes faster and more efficient, the core lessons remain the same—trust your instincts, verify your partners, and always prioritize your customers.

Community Building Tips

Build partnerships with organizations that align with your values, such as the performance-handicapped fulfillment center I worked with.

Foster relationships with customers by providing transparent communication during crises. A loyal community can help mitigate bad publicity and support recovery efforts.

Reflection on Passing Down Knowledge

This venture reinforced the importance of passing down hard-earned lessons. Sharing insights about diligence, adaptability, and customer relations can prepare the next generation of entrepreneurs for the challenges they will inevitably face.

Action Steps for New Entrepreneurs

- **Vet Every Partner Thoroughly**: Ensure they can deliver on promises and have backup plans if they fail.
- **Understand the Laws**: Learn the legalities of your business model, and don't cut corners.
- **Be Prepared to Pivot**: Stay flexible and open to alternative paths if the original idea doesn't work.
- **Prioritize Customer Communication**: Transparency during problems can help maintain trust and salvage your reputation.

Think About This
- How do you determine when to pivot your business strategy in response to changing market trends?
- What steps do you take to ensure your products or services remain relevant to your target audience?
- Can you recall a time when you had to innovate to stay competitive? What was the outcome?

How Would This Apply to You?
- Regularly assess market trends and be prepared to adapt your offerings to meet evolving customer preferences.
- Encourage a culture of innovation within your team to foster creative solutions and maintain a competitive edge.
- Develop a contingency plan that allows for flexibility in your business operations during times of change.

"Innovation distinguishes between a leader and a follower."

- Steve Jobs
Apple

#9

Western College of Criminology

In the evolving field of criminal justice education, the Western College of Criminology was a leader in innovation and excellence. Its programs combined theoretical knowledge with practical skills for real-world application, fostering critical thinking and ethical practices that set a high standard in criminology.

As mentioned in an earlier chapter, I was always fascinated by police work as a kid. I spent countless hours at the library, absorbing everything I could about law enforcement, from investigative procedures to forensics. Although I was rejected as a police cadet at 15, years later I had the opportunity to obtain the marketing rights to the Western College of Criminology in Los Angeles. The college was a well-established business with a large guard service and a post-secondary educational unit that offered certification in various criminal justice fields.

In the early 1980s, tear gas was being promoted as an effective self-defense product. Sensing a trend, I saw an opportunity to develop a tear gas training program alongside the sale of the product. I took the necessary legal steps, including obtaining state licensing and Department of Justice certification. After purchasing the marketing rights for $10,000, I created a comprehensive training, sales, and marketing program, complete with classroom instruction and manuals.

We advertised the classes, offering training and certification to the public for a nominal fee. The product quickly gained public interest, driven by

Key Takeaways from
Western College of Criminology

The experience of marketing the Western College of Criminology, combined with the tear gas training program, reinforced the importance of understanding a product's true capabilities and limitations. What seemed like a promising self-defense tool ultimately fell short due to real-world challenges, offering key lessons in product evaluation and consumer safety.

Due Diligence Is Non-Negotiable

Before investing in a product, thoroughly research and test it in real-world conditions. Tear gas performed well for law enforcement but failed for average users. Lesson: rigorously test effectiveness in customer scenarios.

The Importance of Meeting Consumer Needs

The tear gas product was a great concept, but it didn't fit the reality of what the public needed for self-defense. Just because a product works in theory doesn't mean it will succeed in practice. The success of any product lies in how well it meets the real-world needs of its users, especially in safety-related industries.

Anticipating Public and Media Scrutiny

When a product deals with personal safety, public scrutiny is inevitable. Investigative reporters and dissatisfied customers were quick to expose the tear gas product's shortcomings, and this public attention brought the project to a halt. The takeaway: be prepared for public feedback and media inquiries by ensuring that your product holds up to scrutiny from the very beginning.

Practical Advice for Modern Entrepreneurs

Test Products in Real-World Conditions: Before releasing any product, especially one related to safety, test it thoroughly in real-world situations. Make sure it meets the needs of its intended users.

Align Products with Consumer Expectations: A product's effectiveness depends on how well it serves its audience. Even the best ideas will fail if they don't meet practical consumer needs.

Prepare for Public Scrutiny: In the age of instant feedback and media coverage, ensure your product can withstand criticism. Be ready for questions and concerns by addressing potential limitations up front.

Action Steps for New Entrepreneurs

- **Conduct Rigorous Product Testing**: Don't rely on controlled environments. Test your product under real-world conditions to see if it meets the demands of everyday users.

- **Focus on the End User**: Always ask, "Will this work for my target audience in real-life situations?" A great concept isn't enough—practical application is key.

- **Expect and Address Criticism**: Be transparent about your product's limitations from the start. Prepare for media or public scrutiny by ensuring your product is as strong as possible.

Think About This

- How do educational institutions influence the evolution of criminal justice practices?

- What role does ethics play in the curriculum of criminology programs?

- How can colleges balance theoretical instruction with practical experience in criminal justice education?

How Would This Apply to You?

- Reflect on the importance of ethics in your professional development within the field of criminology.

- Consider ways to integrate practical experiences, such as internships or simulations, into your educational journey.

- Identify opportunities to engage with contemporary issues in criminal justice through academic research or community involvement.

> "Education is the most powerful weapon which you can use to change the world."
>
> - *Nelson Mandela*
> *President of South Africa*

#10
Start Me Up Auto Product

In the competitive automotive industry, innovation is key. David's venture into the "Start Me Up" auto product aimed to revolutionize vehicle maintenance. However, the journey underscored the importance of thorough market research and understanding consumer behavior.

After the failure of my earlier Sure Safe auto product, you'd think I would have learned my lesson. But, driven by greed and the hope of redemption, I decided to give the auto industry another shot. We had been doing some contract sub-assembly work for a local nonprofit organization for disabled people when I met an individual with an inventive and futuristic mindset. He had developed a circuit board that, under the right circumstances, could give a car battery an instant charge.

The idea seemed simple: a stranded motorist with a dead battery could plug this unit into the cigarette lighter and receive just enough power to crank the engine a few times and get the car started. For me, this was creative nirvana. We began assembling the product and put together a marketing plan.

To bring this idea to life, I formed a partnership with a friend who had a PhD and an MBA. We decided to target women specifically, reasoning that men would prefer traditional battery cables, while our ergonomically designed handheld unit would appeal to women. The circuitry was already in place and tested, but we needed a reliable battery source. We found it in the soon-to-be-extinct Polaroid Corporation, which had millions of leftover batteries from their old Polaroid land cameras. These wafer-thin square batteries were perfect for our needs.

Unfortunately, we were undercapitalized from the start, a common and often fatal issue. Polaroid agreed to provide the batteries on consignment, but they wanted to handle the marketing. In our eagerness to get going, we set up a 3,000-square-foot facility in an industrial park and began producing the product with a crew of 200 home-based workers. We produced over 300,000 units.

However, there was a critical marketing misstep. Despite my experience in the cosmetic industry, where I knew this was a product for women, Polaroid pushed it through their male-dominated distribution channels. As a result, the product never gained traction. Despite exposure on QVC and even Oprah, the market soon filled with competing products from auto, insurance, and aftermarket companies, and our product faded into obscurity.

What I Learned

I learned that even the best ideas can fail if they're undercapitalized and marketed incorrectly. It's essential to understand your target audience and ensure your marketing partners are aligned with that vision.

My biggest lesson was that insufficient capital and a flawed marketing strategy can doom a project, no matter how good the idea. The right idea, aimed at the wrong market, will still fail.

Key Takeaways from
Start Me Up Auto Product

The Start Me Up Auto Product was an exciting, innovative idea created to help motorists with dead car batteries. However, like many ideas, it ultimately fell short due to poor execution, undercapitalization, and a critical misstep in targeting the wrong market. This venture was a hard lesson in balancing creativity with essential business fundamentals.

Innovation Alone Is Not Enough

The concept of a small, user-friendly device that could provide an instant charge through a car's cigarette lighter was revolutionary at the time. But innovation alone doesn't guarantee success. While the product had potential, it needed more than just a creative spark—it required careful planning, the right partnerships, and a sound strategy. The lesson here is that creativity, without a strong foundation of capital and market understanding, often leads to failure.

Understand the Importance of Proper Capitalization

From the beginning, we were undercapitalized, a common issue for many startups. While Polaroid agreed to provide batteries on consignment, that wasn't enough to cover the costs of marketing, distribution, and competing in an industry full of well-established players. The lack of financial backing meant we couldn't properly sustain or grow the business. The key lesson is that great ideas need adequate funding—not just for production but for marketing, scaling, and adjusting to market demands.

Misalignment with Marketing Partners Can Derail Success

Despite my experience in the cosmetic industry, where I learned that certain products appeal more to specific demographics, I allowed Polaroid to push our product through their male-dominated channels, neglecting the original vision to target women. The ergonomic design and the ease of use were meant to appeal specifically to female motorists, but Polaroid's marketing channels, deeply embedded in the male-driven auto industry, failed to reach the intended audience. The result? The product never gained traction. Marketing misalignment can be a silent killer and ensuring that your partners share your vision is essential to success.

Timing and Market Competition Matter

Although we had initial exposure on platforms like QVC and even Oprah, the automotive and aftermarket industries soon flooded the market with competing products. Our failure to anticipate this competition and prepare for it—by differentiating our product more effectively or adjusting our marketing strategy—meant we were outpaced. Timing in business is critical. Launching a product without considering potential market shifts can leave even a great idea behind.

Don't Let Desperation Drive Decisions

I was driven by a desire to redeem myself after the failure of the *Sure Safe* product. That urgency led me to ignore warning signs and move forward with undercapitalization, poor marketing alignment, and without fully thinking through the competitive landscape. The need for redemption blinded me to critical flaws in the plan. This taught me that desperation is a dangerous motivator. Business decisions must be made from a place of strategy, not from a desire to prove something.

Practical Advice for Modern Entrepreneurs: Capitalize Properly from the Start

Before launching, ensure you have enough financial backing to handle production, marketing, and unforeseen challenges. Lack of capital is a major cause of failure for even the most innovative products.

Target the Right Audience: Clearly define your target demographic and ensure your marketing and distribution channels align with that audience. Mismatched marketing strategies can doom a product.

Be Ready for Competition: No matter how unique your idea seems, anticipate market competition. Differentiate your product early and plan how to stand out in a crowded field.

Don't Let Redemption Be Your Driver: Never make decisions based on a need to fix past mistakes. Approach every venture with clear eyes and strategic thinking, not emotional reactions.

Action Steps for New Entrepreneurs

- **Ensure Proper Capitalization**: Don't rely on partial funding. Make sure you have the capital needed to sustain production, marketing, and any unexpected costs.

- **Align Marketing with Your Vision**: Carefully choose marketing partners who share your vision and will reach your intended audience effectively. Don't compromise your target market for ease of distribution.

- **Anticipate Market Shifts**: Always assume competitors will enter the market. Have a plan in place for how you'll differentiate your product once others arrive.

- **Make Decisions Based on Strategy, Not Emotion**: Focus on careful planning and strategic moves rather than being driven by a need to redeem yourself or outdo a past failure.

Think About This
- How do you assess the demand for a new product in a saturated market?
- What strategies do you employ to differentiate your product from competitors?
- Can you recall a time when market feedback led you to pivot your business approach? What did you learn?

How Would This Apply to You?

- Conduct comprehensive market research to identify gaps and opportunities before launching a new product.
- Develop a unique value proposition that clearly communicates the benefits of your product to potential customers.
- Be prepared to adapt your business strategy based on consumer feedback and market trends.

"Sometimes your best investments are the ones you don't make."

- Donald Trump
45th and 47th President of the United States
Trump Organization

#11
Nothing Down Real Estate

In the world of real estate, the phrase "nothing down" sounds almost too good to be true. Yet, David managed to turn this unconventional approach into a profitable strategy, completing 22 deals and earning over $750,000 in two years. But behind the numbers lay a series of lessons about creativity, resilience, and the art of negotiation.

Following the collapse of the restaurant business in Lake Tahoe, we moved back to the Thousand Oaks area. It was perhaps the most difficult time in our married life due to financial strain and essentially the loss of everything we had ever worked for. Divine intervention and the law of attraction once again played a major role in my life. My wife found and bought a book for $9.95 about nothing down real estate. We devoured its contents and, with a high level of skepticism, began to seriously explore the possibility of making the concepts in the book work. After all, the author was a nationally recognized expert and a published author with a #1 national best seller about nothing down real estate. What follows is Robert Allen's story about our entry into and involvement in this niche market of the real estate industry.

The Real Estate Journey Begins

In the introduction to his best-selling book *Nothing Down for the 2000's*, Robert Allen writes about second chances. Having survived the trauma of a serious automobile accident, knowing that he was seconds away from death, Robert learned how important second chances can be. Many of his most successful students are like him— second chancers, driven by deep purpose. Sonja and I were two such students. Over time, we racked up an incredible twenty-two "nothing down" deals within our first two years of real estate investing, becoming real estate multi-millionaires.

I grew up in England during World War II. My beginnings were very humble. I lived in a state of abject poverty in a thatched hut—nothing like the charming ones Thomas

Kincaid paints, but rather a rat-infested hovel with no electricity, no running water, and only one cooked meal each week. It was an incredibly negative upbringing, but it shaped my hunger for something better.

After graduating from Bridgewater Technical Institute, I immigrated to Canada at the age of fifteen, studied economics at the University of British Columbia, and later moved to the United States. There, I spent twenty-five years in sales and international management positions with companies like Revlon, Helena Rubinstein, Lancôme, and Charles of the Ritz. Eventually, I ventured into entrepreneurship, owning sixteen businesses ranging from restaurants to manufacturing.

A Family Crisis Changes Everything

It was during this entrepreneurial phase that our lives were dramatically impacted by a family crisis. Our son, Steven, had joined the U.S. Air Force and was shipped off to a tactical nuclear airbase in Germany, where his work involved chemical washes on tactical nuclear bombs. Eighteen months into his service, we received a phone call from Steven. His voice was barely audible—he was gravely ill. He had been struck by sudden, excruciating pain, and after months of misdiagnoses, including appendicitis and even AIDS, Steven's condition worsened daily. Eventually, the doctors diagnosed him with Varicella Zoster, a dangerous form of shingles that attacked his bladder and caused severe nerve damage.

My wife Sonja flew to Germany immediately. She watched helplessly as Steven, strapped to a gurney, was tortured by unspeakable pain. The morphine shots he was given only seemed to add to his discomfort. Eventually, after three months, a staff internist correctly diagnosed Steven, but by then it was too late—Steven was permanently disabled. His condition was rapidly deteriorating.

I made an impassioned plea to the base commander to transfer Steven back to the U.S. for proper treatment, but my request was arrogantly denied. I stormed into my congressman's office, vented my frustration, and within 24 hours, the Secretary of the Air Force had arranged for Steven to be transported back to the U.S. While this was a victory, our battle was far from over. It took fifteen more years, thirty-seven hospitalizations, and countless legal battles with the Veterans Administration before Steven was finally granted his pension. The experience left us financially, emotionally, and physically devastated.

A New Opportunity

After years of entrepreneurial ventures that had provided millions for the fight but not for the future, we found ourselves in desperate need of something that would work for us now. That's when we discovered Robert Allen's *Nothing Down* real estate program. It was exactly what we needed—our second chance.

We started attending real estate seminars, including one in Las Vegas hosted by Robert Allen himself. I was impressed by his demonstration of commitment, and Sonja and I began devouring every one of his books. What struck me most was not just the technical skills but the release of potential within myself. I had grown up with such a negative upbringing, but this new venture released something powerful within me.

In less than two years, we completed 22 "nothing down" real estate deals, sold over $3 million worth of property, and made a personal profit of over $750,000. We had cracked the code to ultimate wealth using a cookie-cutter approach. We carefully crafted an advertisement that ran in local newspapers for just $157 a month, which brought sellers to us. We developed a system where we would meet with sellers, establish trust, and understand their needs, often spending several hours at their homes before closing a deal.

Lessons from the Field

We learned that success in real estate comes from understanding people's challenges. By becoming students of the sellers, we could apply what we learned to meet their needs and close deals. One key piece of advice I give to new investors is this: Don't let ambition and greed override the laws of real estate. If a deal seems shady, back away. If it requires bending the rules, don't go there.

We also learned that systems are vital for success. We developed strict systems for everything, from screening tenants to ensuring that subcontractors met deadlines. In one case, we failed to pull a credit report on a tenant, which resulted in an eviction. After that experience, we never skipped that crucial step again.

Expanding the Vision

With the collapse of the real estate market and the loss of substantial equity during the 2008 crash, Sonja and I shifted our focus from single-family homes to developing affordable senior housing communities. Our vision was to build a national chain of 100-acre senior manufactured housing parks, providing dignified, affordable housing to one million seniors within ten years. Site acquisition is already underway in several states, including AZ, CA and FL.

What I Learned:
- Real estate success is not just about technical knowledge but also about understanding people. Trust, relationships, and a commitment to ethical practices are paramount.

- Systems and discipline are crucial for managing multiple deals effectively. Screening tenants, managing hold times, and enforcing deadlines with subcontractors ensure long-term profitability.

My Biggest Lesson: The biggest lesson I learned was that personal resilience is as important as business strategy. Our journey, particularly through the challenges of our son's health crisis, taught me that persistence and an unwavering focus on your goals are critical to success, no matter what obstacles stand in your way.

Key Takeaways
from Nothing Down Real Estate

The *Nothing Down Real Estate* venture came during one of the most challenging times in my life, both personally and financially. After experiencing immense hardship and loss, my wife and I found a second chance in real estate investment. This venture taught me not just about business strategy but about the power of persistence, relationships, and developing systems for long-term success.

Understanding People
is the Key to Real Estate Success

The heart of real estate lies not just in the properties but in the people behind the deals. What made our approach successful was our ability to understand the needs, challenges, and emotional state of sellers. We spent hours building trust, asking questions, and offering solutions that met their needs. Real estate isn't just about numbers—it's about relationships. The lesson here is that if you take the time to connect with people, you can structure deals that are win-win for both sides. Emotional intelligence and empathy are as valuable as technical real estate knowledge.

Systems and Discipline Drive Consistency

With 22 deals completed in two years, having solid systems in place was critical. Whether it was tenant screening, managing timelines with subcontractors, or developing strict processes for each part of the deal, these systems ensured that we didn't miss crucial steps. The one time we failed to follow our own pro- cess, by skipping a credit check on a tenant, it led to a costly eviction. That mistake reinforced the import- ance of discipline in real estate. Systems aren't just about efficiency; they are about protecting your investments.

Resilience is Just as Important as Strategy

At the core of our success wasn't just the technical knowledge we gained from Robert Allen's program—it was our resilience. After losing everything from our previous ventures, facing financial strain, and enduring our son's health crisis, real estate became our lifeline. The ability to persist through personal hardship, stay focused on long-term goals, and overcome adversity was the true driver of our success. The biggest lesson here? In business and in life, your ability to stay resilient and keep going despite setbacks is often more valuable than any strategy.

Don't Let Greed or Ambition Compromise Ethics

One of the most critical lessons I learned was the importance of ethics in real estate. While profit is tempting, we always backed away from deals that felt shady or required bending rules. Real success comes from building trust and maintaining integrity. Cutting corners may bring short-term gains but can harm your reputation and long-term success.

Practical Advice for Modern Entrepreneurs

Master Relationship Building: Real estate is more about people than properties. Focus on building trust and understanding the needs of the people you're working with. Deals are often sealed because of the relationship, not just the numbers.

Develop and Stick to Systems: Implement systems for tenant screening, deal timelines, and managing contractors. Discipline in following these systems will help avoid costly mistakes.

Prepare for Setbacks: Success doesn't come without challenges. Develop personal resilience and be prepared to face adversity with persistence and focus.

Practice Ethical Business: Don't let ambition or desperation push you into unethical decisions. Always prioritize long-term integrity over short-term profit.

Action Steps for New Entrepreneurs

- **Focus on Understanding People:** Take the time to ask questions and understand the emotional and practical needs of those involved in your deals. Building strong relationships will yield more success than just chasing numbers.

- **Build Solid Systems:** Create repeatable processes for every step in your business. Whether it's screening tenants or managing deadlines, systems protect you from preventable mistakes.

- **Cultivate Resilience:** Develop the ability to bounce back from setbacks. Real estate, like any business, is full of ups and downs, and resilience will keep you moving forward.

- **Stay Ethical:** Never compromise on your values or integrity for the sake of a deal. In the long run, your reputation is worth more than any single transaction.

Think About This

- How do you approach opportunities that seem unconventional or outside the norm?

- What strategies have you used to minimize risk in business ventures?

- When have you relied on creativity to overcome a financial or logistical challenge?

How Would This Apply to You?

- Identify one unconventional approach or idea you've considered. What would it take to turn it into a viable opportunity?

- Reflect on your current investments or projects. How can you better minimize risk without limiting potential rewards*?*

- Think of a negotiation you're currently facing. How can you leverage creativity to achieve a win-win outcome?

> "The first man gets the oyster,
> the second man gets the shell.
>
> *- Andrew Carnegie*
> *Carnegie Steel Company*

#12 SENIOR PARKS USA

Envision a community where seniors enjoy affordable, dignified housing tailored to their needs.
Senior Parks USA aims to transform this vision into reality, offering ergonomically designed homes within vibrant, supportive environments. But what challenges arise in creating such ideal communities?

www.seniorparksusa.com

In 2005, I enrolled in a seminar sponsored by Mark Victor Hansen and Robert Allen. In addition to the price of admission, each of the 38 attendees had to bring three "million-dollar ideas" in written form. Those three days turned out to be the most important educational experience of my life, proving that the best investment you can make is in your personal development.

We are taught to go to school, get a good education, secure a stable job, and live happily ever after. While education is important, it must also foster creative thought. Times have changed, and this old formula no longer guarantees success, but many people, like me, still carry self-limiting beliefs that hinder creativity. Over the course of the seminar, I realized that many of the beliefs instilled by the traditional education system—designed by industry to produce skilled employees—can create mental blocks and conflicts. When conflict exists, congruency cannot.

This seminar was all about breaking through those limitations. Each participant presented their million-dollar ideas, which were evaluated by the group based on need, feasibility, and timing. At the conclusion of the event, Mark Victor Hansen said to me, "David, your idea of senior parks is not a million-dollar idea; it's a billion-dollar idea."

The Birth of Senior Parks USA

It took many years for me to cross the mental bridge of fear and finally pursue this project, but now it's truly under way, and I feel a sense of fulfillment and excitement for the future as never before. I believe this project will outlive me and provide significant help to seniors across the country.

The concept for Senior Parks USA had its beginnings in my mother's cottage in Bishops Lydeard, Somerset, England. Her 750-square-foot, two-bedroom, one-bath home was part of a community where seniors lived in privacy but had a strong sense of connection to their neighbors. In her village, dozens of cottages were clustered together, and everyone was within walking distance of one another.

Inspired by this, I envisioned an entire village of about 400 homes on approximately 100 acres, complete with all the amenities seniors need and desire—community centers, a general store, recreational activities like a putting green, and more. These parks would provide a self-sustaining, supportive collection of resources at a much more affordable price than the high-end "senior retirement homes" that charge $5,000 to $9,000 per month.

In those high-end homes, residents are essentially renting 1, 2, or 3-bedroom apartments and receiving meals, entertainment, and the services of an activity director. My vision is different: in Senior Parks USA, each cottage would be a free-standing home, owned by the occupant, offering the same lifestyle benefits but at a more affordable price. Basic medical care and limited assisted living would also be available.

Launching the Vision

As of 2024, plans for the first Senior Parks pilot village are underway, with initial locations planned in Hawaii and Fort Worth, Texas. The goal is to expand from there as we gain experience and grow. The project is structured as a 501(c)(3) nonprofit organization, ensuring that it remains focused on its mission to provide affordable, dignified housing for seniors.

A comprehensive marketing plan is in development, and there will be a massive media campaign to engage senior organizations, civic groups, municipalities, veterans, and state, county, and federal agencies. The plan is to present at annual governor and mayor conferences to spread national awareness of the urgent need for affordable housing for seniors.

What I Learned:

- The importance of personal development cannot be overstated. Even after years of success, continuing to invest in learning and self-growth opens doors to new opportunities.

- Ideas that seem impossible at first can become reality with persistence and belief in their potential. The journey from idea to execution is long but worth the effort.

My Biggest Lesson: Fear and self-limiting beliefs are the biggest obstacles to success. Once I broke free of the mindset that held me back, I was able to launch a project that has the potential to help millions of seniors live with dignity and independence in their later years. The only limits are the ones we place on ourselves.

Key Takeaways from Senior Parks USA

The journey of launching *Senior Parks USA* has been deeply rewarding, revealing new ways to approach both business and life. This venture wasn't just about creating a profitable business—it was about serving a real need, building something that could outlast me, and overcoming personal limitations. Here are the most valuable lessons from this experience.

Big Ideas Need Time to Mature— But Take the First Step

Great ideas, like *Senior Parks USA*, often sit in the back of our minds because of fear, doubt, or self-limiting beliefs. It took me years to finally act on this project, but once I did, the momentum built quickly. The key lesson is this: you don't need to have everything figured out to start. The first step will create its own momentum, and clarity will come as you move forward. The takeaway? Don't wait until the perfect time—take action and let the idea evolve.

Your Past Can Shape Your Vision

This venture was inspired by a personal experience with my mother's cottage community in England. Sometimes, the seeds of your next big project are already in your past, waiting to be recognized. By reflecting on your own experiences, especially those that made a lasting impact—you can find unique and valuable insights for future business ventures. My advice is to tap into personal stories and memories when crafting your vision. It adds authenticity and heart to what you're building.

Solving a Real Problem
Beats Following Trends

Instead of chasing hot business trends, focus on addressing real, enduring problems. *Senior Parks USA* was born from recognizing the deep need for affordable, dignified senior housing, rather than chasing the latest fad. The lesson here is that the most impactful businesses often solve long-term challenges, not temporary trends. Identify a problem that truly matters, and you'll always have demand.

Mission-Driven Ventures
Attract Like-Minded Partners

Building *Senior Parks USA* as a nonprofit allowed us to focus on the mission of providing affordable senior housing, attracting partners who share that same vision. This wasn't just about making money—it was about creating something that would benefit people long after I'm gone. When your business is aligned with a larger purpose, you attract passionate people who can help amplify your vision. It's a powerful way to ensure that your project has long-term sustainability and impact.

Practical Advice for
Modern Entrepreneurs

Don't Wait for Perfection: If you're passionate about an idea, start now. The first step doesn't have to be perfect, but it will create momentum and help the idea take shape.

Leverage Your Personal Story: Reflect on your life experiences, they can provide unique insights and shape your business in ways that resonate deeply with others.

Solve Big Problems: Instead of chasing the latest business trends, focus on solving real, enduring challenges. Businesses that provide long-term solutions are often the most successful.

Build Around a Mission: If your business serves a larger purpose, make that your focus. A mission-driven business attracts like-minded partners who will help you achieve your goals.

Action Steps for New Entrepreneurs

- **Start Before You're Ready**: Don't wait for all the pieces to be in place. Act now and let the journey unfold.

- **Reflect on Your Past**: Tap into personal experiences that have shaped you and let them inspire your vision.

- **Identify a Meaningful Problem to Solve**: Focus on creating a solution to a real, lasting problem will ensure your business remains relevant and valuable.

- **Align with a Larger Mission**: Structure your business around a mission that matters. Purpose-driven ventures attract passionate people and create lasting impact.

This version is designed to offer more unique advice and insight while avoiding redundancy from previous ventures.

Think About This
- How do you balance affordability with quality when developing housing for seniors?
- What amenities are essential to foster a sense of community and well-being among residents?
- How can sustainable and energy-efficient designs be integrated into senior housing developments?

How Would This Apply to You?
- Identify ways to incorporate universal design principles to enhance accessibility in your living or working spaces.
- Consider how community engagement and social activities can be promoted within your neighborhood or organization.
- Explore opportunities to implement sustainable practices in your environment to benefit both residents and the planet.

#13

International Entrepreneurs Association

Empowering Global Visionaries

*What if you could harness the collective
ingenuity of entrepreneurs from every
corner of the globe?*
*The International Entrepreneurs Association (IEA)
brings this vision to life. More than a network, it's a
movement—a dynamic force where innovation
transcends borders, and global challenges meet
entrepreneurial solutions.*
*The IEA isn't just about shaping businesses;
it's about shaping the future.*

www.IEA777.com

PRESS RELEASE FOR IMMEDIATE RELEASE
International Entrepreneurs Association to Execute a Soft Launch

United States, August 02, 2024 –
The International Entrepreneurs Association (IEA) is an organization built around the idea that today's young entrepreneurs can pool their experiences and share them with millions of others who also wish to build small enterprises or businesses for themselves and their families. The IEA's marketing plan will kick off with a soft launch, enabling the organization's initial members to try out the program before additional features and achievement levels are introduced.

Currently, the IEA is in its development stage and aims to provide guidance and direction through a network of licensed Executive Director mentors in each country. The initial focus for the Executive Directors will be on import/export for immediate revenue generation. The founder and CEO, David Selley, based in Hawaii, stated in a memo: "As an entrepreneur with many years of experience, I have extensively studied the 'entrepreneur market' and its commercial potential, which is why I founded the International Entrepreneurs Association."

Mr. Selley goes on to explain the enormous potential of the entrepreneur market, estimated to include over 700 million people globally. He believes that many individuals now recognize that their true income potential does not have to come from adhering to the directions, rules, and regulations of traditional organizations. According to

Selley, to succeed as an entrepreneur, one must have a clear sense of their goals and how best to achieve them. The IEA's mission is to provide the combined knowledge and extensive resources needed to help entrepreneurs around the world realize their potential.

Membership Benefits Include:

1. Membership in a worldwide association.

2. Access to experienced, qualified Executive Directors who are dedicated to supporting you, as well as resources from the IEA website.

3. Guidance on how to protect your ideas.

4. Training on how to become a successful entrepreneur.

5. Opportunities to attend local, national, and international IEA events.

6. An IEA membership certificate and basic training manual.

7. Monthly learning challenges to engage with if desired.

8. Assistance in obtaining venture capital.

9. Ability to market and sell your ideas through the IEA website.

10. Guidance on conducting market research or finding the right resources.

11. Participation in local, regional, national, and international webinars.

12. Access to fee-based international webinars featuring world-renowned speakers.

13. Participation in the IEA blog to engage with the community.

14. A portion of your member fee will be donated to a local charity selected by your Executive Director.

15. Invitations to local, regional, and national events in your country.

16. The opportunity to apply for an IEA chapter in your area to develop networking opportunities.

17. Access to limited Executive Director positions.

18. Membership in the IEA LinkedIn group.

19. Special industry alerts with insider access to opportunities.

20. Opportunity to create and participate in mastermind groups.

21. Open access to IEA leadership and headquarters.

MOTTO: WIN-WIN for everyone

Soft Launch and Expansion

The IEA's soft launch will initially target 50 major cities in 30 countries, including the United States, the United Kingdom, Canada, China, India, Thailand, and Nigeria. These markets were chosen due to their robust growth in entrepreneurship. To promote the IEA's expansion, the organization will also publish target-specific books that highlight local businesses and entrepreneurs.

Looking ahead, Selley anticipates significant vertical growth, allowing the IEA to transition into licensing member countries, states, and regions. Applicants interested in becoming IEA licensees will need to meet specific requirements to ensure the success of their market areas.

While the IEA is still in its early stages, Selley remains optimistic about its potential to unite brilliant entrepreneurial minds and help usher in a better world.

What I Learned

- The entrepreneurial market is vast, with millions of people looking for ways to break free from traditional employment. It's essential to provide accessible guidance, resources, and a support network to help aspiring entrepreneurs succeed.

- Timing and innovation are critical. Launching the International Entrepreneurs Association with a focus on global mentoring and knowledge sharing can create lasting impact and empower a new generation of business leaders.

My Biggest Lesson

- The key to success is collaboration. By pooling knowledge and sharing experiences, entrepreneurs can overcome challenges and achieve their goals more efficiently. Through the IEA, we aim to create a global community where everyone benefits from each other's wisdom, skills, and insights. This creates a win-win environment that fosters growth for all participants.

Think About This

- How often do you connect with like-minded individuals to share ideas and collaborate?

- Are you leveraging global trends and perspectives to stay ahead in your industry?

- What tools or networks could help you expand your business beyond local or national boundaries?

How Would This Apply to You?

- **Build a Global Network:** Join communities that expand your reach and expose you to diverse business practices.

- **Stay Ahead of Trends:** Regularly update your knowledge of global markets to identify emerging opportunities.

- **Collaborate Across Borders:** Explore partnerships with entrepreneurs worldwide to innovate and grow.

"Entrepreneurship knows no borders—
it thrives on the power of
global connections and shared ambitions."

- David Selley
Entrepreneur, Author

#14 Famous 50 Book Series
(A vanity publishing series)

What does it mean to stand among the best?
The Famous 50 Book Series dares to answer that
question, spotlighting extraordinary individuals whose
achievements redefine excellence in their fields. Each
volume invites readers to explore the untold stories,
groundbreaking ideas, and bold journeys that set these
professionals apart. For the contributors,
it's not just a feature—it's a legacy.

© 2016

www.famous50.com

The **FAMOUS 50** book series is an exciting project in process, designed as an attractive sales and public relations tool for various industries. It aims to spotlight professionals from over 100 categories such as realtors, bed and breakfasts (B&Bs), spas, hotel chains, entrepreneurs, authors, and more. This vanity publishing series will provide an exceptional opportunity for participants to gain recognition and showcase their expertise in a globally licensed and multi-language format.

Outline of the Project

The **Famous 50** series is structured as a globally licensed program. For a nominal license entry fee and royalty, licensees will have the ability to publish within their country, state, province, territory, or area of specific expertise. For example, a prominent leader in the real estate industry could secure a license and then appear in the book for a modest fee of $50, along with 50 other top professionals from the same category.

Each entry will feature a **four-page spread**, including the participant's **photo, biography, and contact information**. This not only serves as a marketing tool but also provides **territorial protection**, ensuring that entries within specific regions are exclusive.

With the availability of **first and second editions**, the books will gain prestige, providing added value to both participants and readers. Furthermore, all revenues, minus the royalty fee, will go directly to the licensee, making this an appealing venture for those interested in building a globally recognized brand.

The **Famous 50 Book Series** will be available in multiple languages, allowing participants to showcase their achievements on a worldwide platform, creating an expansive network of professionals.

What I Learned

- **Scalability and Global Reach:** By licensing the **Famous 50** series globally, we can reach a vast audience across industries and locations. The model ensures that participants benefit from both local and international exposure, making this a powerful tool for self-promotion and professional recognition.

- **Strategic Value in Vanity Publishing:** Vanity publishing, often misunderstood, can be a highly effective means of personal branding and promotion. By curating a high-quality publication that spotlights professionals, we create a unique opportunity for individuals to market themselves in a format that offers credibility and prestige.

- **Building Strong Networks:** The **Famous 50** series is not just a book; it's a connection point. It helps professionals' network and grow their influence by being featured alongside other leading figures in their industry. This fosters trust and credibility, building solid relationships within their professional community.

My Biggest Lesson

- **Quality Creates Long-Term Value:** Vanity publishing, when done right, offers immense value. In the **Famous 50** series, the focus is not just on creating a book but on ensuring that the participants feel the pride and prestige of being featured. The exclusivity of this project—being one of only 50 professionals in a particular field—creates lasting value for those involved, helping them stand out in their industries and enhance their professional reputations.

Think About This

- What makes you stand out in your industry. field?
- How would being featured alongside other top professionals elevate your credibility?
- What lasting impression do you want to leave with your clients or audience?

How Would This Apply to You?

- **Leverage Prestige:** Being included in the *Famous 50* enhances your professional profile and positions you as a leader in your field.
- **Expand Your Reach:** Use your feature to connect with new clients, collaborators, and markets.
- **Showcase Your Expertise:** Share your story and achievements to inspire others and solidify your reputation as an industry expert.

> "Your story is your legacy—
> let it inspire the world."
>
> - *David Selley*
> *Entrepreneur, Author*

#15 RELATIONSHIPS

David & Sonja
SELLEY

65 Years of Love and Partnership

What if the greatest secret to success wasn't found in boardrooms or bank accounts, but in the quiet moments shared between two people bound by love and ambition?

David and Sonja Selley's 65-year journey together is a living testament to the power of love, resilience, and shared dreams. Marriage is more than a vow—it's a crucible where ambitions are tested, resilience is forged, and true partnership reveals itself. Their enduring relationship inspires The Relationships Project, showing that thriving together requires balance, trust, and a shared vision for the future.

www.happylifeexpert.com

The **Relationships** project, launched under the banner of ***www.happylifeexpert.com***, is designed to be a transformative tool for understanding, nurturing, and improving personal and professional relationships. Whether it's building a strong foundation in marriage, strengthening family bonds, or creating lasting profess-ional connections, the core message focuses on fostering healthy, long-term relationships through clear communi-cation, empathy, and mutual respect.

This book and the accompanying resources are aimed at anyone looking to develop deeper, more meaningful connections with the people around them. Through real-life examples, expert advice, and actionable strategies, **Relationships** help individuals and couples navigate the complexities of human connections.

Outline of the Project

Relationships will provide readers with insights into the essential elements of successful relationships, such as **trust**, **communication**, **shared values**, and **emotional**

intelligence. Each chapter dives deep into a specific aspect of relationships, offering tools and strategies to overcome challenges and strengthen bonds.

Key topics covered include

- **Building Trust**: The foundation of any successful relationship is trust. Learn how to foster trust through transparency and consistent action.

- **Effective Communication**: Miscommunication is a common pitfall in relationships. Understand how to communicate clearly, listen actively, and resolve conflicts with ease.

- **Empathy and Understanding**: Explore the power of empathy in relationships and how to see things from another person's perspective.

- **Balancing Independence and Togetherness**: Discover the importance of maintaining your individuality while building a partnership.

- **Conflict Resolution**: Learn strategies to navigate and resolve disagreements in a way that strengthens relationships.

- **Professional Relationships**: Beyond personal connections, this project also explores how to build strong, lasting professional relationships that lead to success in business and career growth.

The **Relationships** book also includes exercises, reflection prompts, and worksheets to help readers apply the lessons to their own lives and assess their progress over time.

Visit our website *www.happylifeexpert.com* for more information and additional resources such as work-**shops**, **online courses**, and **relationship coaching**. These tools will further support individuals and couples in their journey to build fulfilling and lasting connections. Participants will also have access to an exclusive **online community** where they can share experiences, seek advice, and gain insights from others on a similar journey.

What I Learned

- **Relationships Are the Core of Success**: Whether personal or professional, strong relationships are the cornerstone of success. This project reinforced the understanding that emotional intelligence and empathy are critical to creating lasting bonds that can withstand the challenges life throws at us.

- **Tailoring Solutions to Individuals**: Just as every person is unique, so are their relationships. There is no one-size-fits-all approach, which is why **Relationships** offers diverse tools and techniques that readers can adapt to their personal circumstances. Providing flexibility in solutions helps individuals apply lessons in ways that best suit their needs.

- **The Importance of Ongoing Growth**: Relationships are dynamic, not static. They evolve over time and require constant attention and effort. This book emphasizes continuous growth, communication, and self-awareness as key elements to keeping relationships strong and meaningful.

My Biggest Lesson

- **Self-Reflection is Key to Healthy Relationships**: One of the biggest takeaways from working on this project is the realization that building strong relationships begins with understanding oneself. By encouraging self-reflection and self-awareness, **Relationships** help readers discover the role they play in their relationships, fostering personal growth that enhances every connection they have.

This project has taught me that **the quality of our relationships defines the quality of our lives**, and investing in those relationships is one of the most important things we can do to lead a happy, fulfilled life.

Think About This
- How does your marriage support or challenge your goals?
- Are you prioritizing communication as much as your work?
- Do you and your partner share a unified vision for your future?

How Would This Apply to You?

- **Align Your Goals:** Ensure both partners are on the same page about priorities and aspirations.
- **Create Boundaries:** Protect quality time with your spouse, even in the busiest seasons of life.
- **Support Each Other's Growth:** Celebrate wins together and tackle setbacks as a team.

"A successful marriage isn't built on perfection but on partnership, where two people grow stronger together than they ever could alone."

- David Selley
Entrepreneur, Author

#16 THE ONE DAY EVENT

What if one day could spark new friendships, interests, and lifelong learning? The One-Day Event offers seniors the chance to explore hobbies, discover talents, and connect with others through workshops, discussions, and networking—all in a fun and engaging atmosphere.

www.longliveseniors.com

The One Day Event hosted by **Long Live Seniors** is a unique, interactive experience designed to enrich the lives of seniors by offering valuable resources, expert guidance, and opportunities to connect with others in their community. Focused on promoting health, wellness, and longevity, this event is a one-stop opportunity for seniors and their families to learn, engage, and be inspired.

Event Overview

The One Day Event offers a full day of workshops, seminars, and activities tailored to the needs and interests of seniors. The event is designed to empower seniors by giving them the tools and knowledge they need to live longer, healthier, and more fulfilling lives.

Key features of the event include:

- **Health and Wellness Workshops**: Led by healthcare professionals, these workshops cover essential topics such as nutrition, physical fitness, mental health, and chronic disease management. Seniors will learn practical tips on maintaining a healthy lifestyle, staying active, and improving overall well-being.

- **Financial Planning for Retirement**: Attendees will gain insights into managing their finances in retirement, including budgeting, investing, and estate planning. Expert financial advisors will provide guidance on making the most of retirement savings and planning for future healthcare needs.

- **Tech for Seniors**: A dedicated session to help seniors stay connected in today's digital world. Attendees will learn how to use smartphones, tablets, and social media to stay in touch with family and friends, manage health appointments, and engage in online communities.

- **Legal Resources and Advice**: Legal experts will be on hand to answer questions about estate planning, wills, and trusts, ensuring seniors are well-prepared for the future. Topics include creating living wills, power of attorney, and understanding legal rights for seniors.

- **Community Networking**: The event provides ample opportunity for seniors to connect with peers, share experiences, and build lasting friendships. Special breakout sessions encourage interaction and create a sense of community among attendees.

- **Activities and Entertainment**: To keep the day lively, the event will feature various interactive activities such as fitness demonstrations, arts and crafts sessions, and live music. Seniors can participate in activities that not only engage their minds and bodies but also bring joy and fun to the day.

- **Resource Fair**: A resource fair with booths and exhibits from senior living communities, healthcare providers, non-profit organizations, and local businesses will be available throughout the day. Attendees can explore the services and support available to them in their local community.

What Makes This Event Special?

The **One Day Event** stands out because it offers a holistic approach to senior well-being. Rather than focusing on one aspect of aging, the event addresses all key areas of life—health, finance, social interaction, and personal growth—giving seniors the tools they need to thrive in their later years.

The event's purpose is to inspire seniors to take control of their future, stay active and engaged, and build lasting relationships in their community. It is a celebration of the senior years, highlighting that aging can be a time of opportunity, discovery, and joy.

How to Participate

To attend **The One Day Event,**
seniors and their families can register online at

www.longliveseniors.com

The website will also feature event schedules, speaker information, and additional resources for attendees. For those unable to attend in person, select sessions will be live-streamed and available for later viewing online.

What I Learned

- **Seniors Need Comprehensive Support**: One of the key takeaways from planning **The One Day Event** is that seniors need access to diverse resources. Health, finances, and social connection are equally important, and creating an event that covers all these areas ensures that seniors feel supported in every aspect of their lives.

- **Community Matters**: The importance of fostering a sense of community became clear throughout this project. Seniors thrive when they have strong social connections, and events like this provide the perfect opportunity for them to meet new people, share experiences, and build relationships that combat isolation.

My Biggest Lesson

- **Engagement Is Essential**: The biggest lesson learned is that keeping seniors engaged through a variety of activities, workshops, and interactions ensures their participation and enjoyment. It's not just about providing information; it's about creating an experience that is meaningful, enjoyable, and deeply impactful for attendees.

The One Day Event is designed to do just that—engage, educate, and empower seniors to live their best lives.

Think About This
- What new skills or hobbies have you always wanted to explore?
- How often do you take time to connect with others and share experiences?
- Are you ready to step out of routine and embrace a day filled with new possibilities?

How Would This Apply to You?
- **Find Your Passion:** Use this event as a chance to uncover interests you've never explored.
- **Build Connections:** Meet like-minded people and create bonds that go beyond the event.
- **Stay Engaged:** Enjoy opportunities to learn, create, and grow in ways that keep life exciting and fulfilling.

> "Adventure doesn't stop with age—
> it begins again with every opportunity
> to learn, connect, and grow."
>
> - David Selley
> Entrepreneur, Author

#17 NETWORK MARKETING

What if your greatest asset in business was already in your hands? Network marketing, or multi-level marketing (MLM), offers a powerful opportunity to turn personal connections into a sustainable income. With low startup costs, flexibility, and the potential for exponential growth, this business model thrives on relationships, trust, and the drive to help others succeed. But success requires more than just joining—it demands strategy, consistency, and the courage to lead.

Network marketing, also known as multi-level marketing (MLM), is a powerful business model that allows individuals to leverage personal relationships and create a self-sustaining income stream. This approach is ideal for people looking to start their own business with low upfront investment while benefiting from established products or services.

The Basics of Network Marketing

Network marketing works by encouraging participants to promote and sell products or services directly to consumers, often through word-of-mouth and personal networks. In addition to retail sales, participants earn income by recruiting others to join the network, building a team, and benefiting from their team's sales.

Key elements of success in network marketing includes:

- **Product or Service Focus**: Network marketing thrives when the products or services offered are high quality and in demand. Participants should believe in the value of the product, as this personal conviction is critical to building trust with potential customers.

- **Duplication and Team Building**: The success of network marketing depends on creating a duplicable system. Participants not only sell products but also recruit others into the business, helping them learn the system and replicate the process. A solid training program and team support are key to growth.

- **Residual Income**: One of the main attractions of network marketing is the potential for residual income. By building a successful downline (team of recruits), participants can earn commissions not just from their direct sales but also from the sales made by their recruits. This creates an opportunity for long-term, sustainable income.

Why Network Marketing Works

Network marketing is popular due to its advantages:

- **Low Start-Up Costs:** Unlike traditional businesses, it requires minimal investment, usually for a starter kit or initial inventory.
- **Flexibility:** Participants can choose their own schedules, working part-time or full-time, making it ideal for stay-at-home parents, retirees, or those seeking additional income.
- **Personal Development:** Companies offer training that enhances skills in sales, leadership, communication, and goal setting, benefiting participants in both business and personal growth.
- **Global Reach:** Digital marketing and social media enable marketers to connect with customers and recruits worldwide, creating vast opportunities for growth and expansion.

Success in Network Marketing

While network marketing offers significant potential,

success requires a dedicated mindset, consistency, and the willingness to learn. Those who succeed often share these common traits:

- **Persistence**: Building a network takes time. Successful network marketers stay focused, even in the face of rejection or slow progress.

- **Leadership**: Being able to inspire and motivate others is crucial in building a strong downline. Leaders must support their teams, providing guidance and encouragement to help them grow.

- **Relationship Building**: Since network marketing thrives on personal relationships, the ability to connect with people is essential. Successful participants invest time in nurturing relationships, understanding customer needs, and building trust.

What I Learned:

- **Leverage Your Network**: The biggest takeaway from network marketing is understanding the power of personal relationships. Success is built on genuine connections, and the more you engage with people, the more opportunities arise for growth.

- **Teach and Duplicate**: Network marketing is all about duplication. Teaching others to do what you do creates exponential growth. The stronger your team, the more residual income and success you'll experience over time.

My Biggest Lesson: Consistency is Key: In network marketing, consistency is crucial. Building a network takes an ongoing effort, but the rewards can be significant with commitment. This applies to expanding your customer base and supporting your team.

Think About This
- Are you leveraging your personal and professional relationships to their fullest potential?
- How well do you support and inspire others to achieve their goals?
- Are you prepared to commit to consistency and long-term growth for sustainable success?

How Would This Apply to You?
- **Build Genuine Connections:** Focus on creating trust and understanding your audience's needs to strengthen your network.
- **Embrace Duplication:** Teach your system to others, enabling your team to grow while you focus on leadership and expansion.
- **Commit to Consistency:** Small, daily actions build momentum and lead to significant long-term rewards.

> "The true power of network marketing lies not just in the income it generates, but in the lives it transforms — yours and those you inspire along the way."
>
> *- David Selley*
> *Entrepreneur, Author*

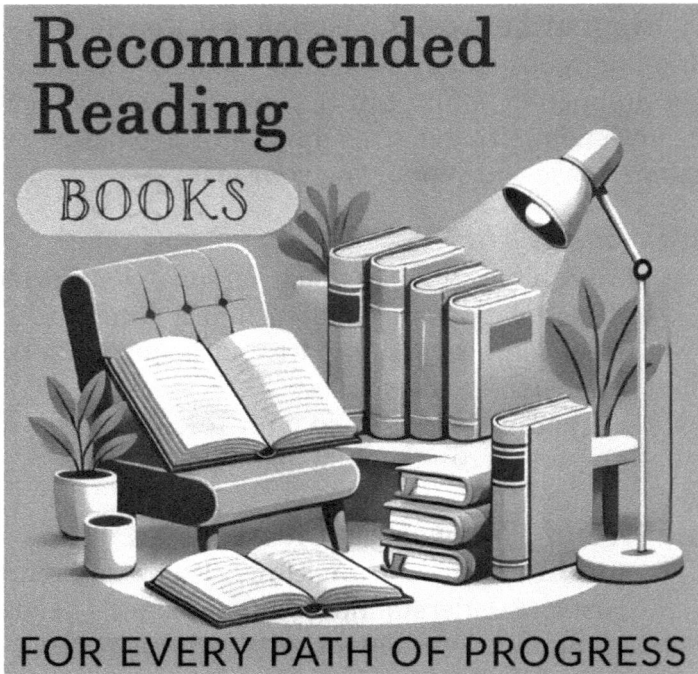

Recommended Reading

BOOKS

FOR EVERY PATH OF PROGRESS

Over the years, I've turned to books for guidance, inspiration, and strategies to overcome challenges and seize opportunities. The titles listed in the following pages have deeply impacted my own entrepreneurial journey, helping me to think differently, act decisively, and grow both personally and professionally. They offer timeless wisdom and practical tools that have been invaluable in shaping my success, and I'm confident they'll provide you with the same inspiration and direction in your pursuits.

#1
Real Estate Investing

1. **"The Millionaire Real Estate Investor"
    by Gary Keller**
    - ○ *Reason*: This book provides a comprehensive guide to real estate investing, from acquiring properties to managing and scaling your portfolio. It offers strategies to become financially independent through real estate, aligning with lessons from David and Sonja's success in leveraging "nothing down" deals.

2. **"Rich Dad Poor Dad" by Robert Kiyosaki**

    - ○ *Reason*: A classic that teaches the importance of financial education and investing in assets like real estate. It emphasizes building passive income, much like the path David and Sonja took when shifting from entrepreneurial ventures to property investments.

#2
Senior Housing and Community Development

1. **"How to Start a Senior Living Business"
    by Tobe Brockner**
    - ○ *Reason*: This book provides insight into creating and managing senior living facilities, in-

cluding market research, financing, and operational planning. It is highly relevant to the vision behind Senior Parks USA, which aims to offer dignified, affordable senior housing.

2. **"The Age of Dignity" by Ai-jen Poo**

    o   *Reason*: This book delves into the care and housing needs of America's aging population. It underscores the growing demand for innovative senior living solutions, aligning with the values of affordable and community-focused senior parks.

#3
Network Marketing

1. **"Go Pro: 7 Steps to Becoming a Network Marketing Professional" by Eric Worre**

    o   *Reason*: This book is a top choice for anyone looking to build a successful network marketing business. It focuses on professional development and gives practical strategies for long-term success in the MLM industry, echoing the importance of systems and personal growth.

2. **"The Four-Year Career" by Richard Bliss Brooke**

    o   *Reason*: This book provides a realistic and inspiring look at what can be achieved in network marketing when the right strategies and dedication are applied. It complements the focus on building residual income and leadership within network marketing.

#4

Entrepreneurship and Mindset

1. **"Think and Grow Rich" by Napoleon Hill**

   o *Reason*: A timeless classic that teaches the power of mindset in achieving financial and personal success. This book aligns with the lessons on personal development, belief systems, and overcoming self-limiting beliefs.

2. **"The Art of the Deal" by Donald J. Trump - 45th & 47th President of the United States**

   o *Reason*: This book offers a behind-the-scenes look at the mindset and strategies behind building a business empire. It emphasizes negotiation skills, strategic thinking, and seizing opportunities, which are fundamental traits for successful entrepreneurs. The lessons align with ventures like Senior Parks USA and The International Entrepreneurs Association, where leadership and innovative thinking drive results.

3. **"The Lean Startup" by Eric Ries**

   o *Reason*: This book is essential for entrepreneurs seeking to launch new ventures with minimal risk. It emphasizes rapid testing and iteration, which aligns with the principles of creativity and adaptability, key themes in the International Entrepreneurs Association.

#5
Marketing and Sales

1. **"Building a StoryBrand: Clarify Your Message So Customers Will Listen" by Donald Miller**

   o *Reason*: This book helps entrepreneurs clarify their message and create marketing that connects with customers. It is ideal for those promoting products or services, such as the Famous 50 Book Series, helping to craft compelling stories for branding and sales.

2. **"Jab, Jab, Jab, Right Hook by Gary Vaynerchuk**

   o *Reason*: This book teaches how to tell your story in a way that resonates across social media platforms. It is highly relevant for those using digital marketing to promote businesses like the International Entrepreneurs Association or Network Marketing endeavors.

#6
Personal Growth and Resilience

1. **"The Power of Now" by Eckhart Tolle**

   o *Reason*: This book teaches the importance of mindfulness and living in the present moment, helping readers manage stress and make clear decisions. It's an excellent resource for overcoming challenges, such as those faced during difficult business transitions.

2. **"Mindset:**
The New Psychology of Success" by Carol S. Dweck

   o *Reason:* This book explains the difference between a fixed and growth mindset. It is essential for entrepreneurs and business owners to adopt resilience and adaptability in the face of setbacks, such as the Lake Tahoe restaurant collapse.

#7
Leadership and Team Building

1. **"Leaders Eat Last" by Simon Sinek**

   o *Reason*: This book focuses on servant leadership, where leaders prioritize their team's well-being. It aligns with the values of developing trust and leadership in ventures like network marketing, senior housing, or entrepreneurship.

2. **"The 5 Levels of Leadership" by John C. Maxwell**

   o *Reason*: This book provides a framework for growing as a leader and inspiring others. It's valuable for managing teams and building successful organizations, such as the International Entrepreneurs Association or real estate investment groups.

#8
Innovation and Business Creativity

1. **"Blue Ocean Strategy" by W. Chan Kim and Renée Mauborgne**

   o *Reason*: This book encourages creating untapped market spaces and avoiding fierce competition by innovating in ways that change the rules of the game. It's ideal for ventures like Senior Parks USA, which aim to meet a growing but underserved market segment.

2. **"Originals: How Non-Conformists Move the World" by Adam Grant**

   o *Reason*: This book is about thinking outside the box and fostering originality in business and life. It resonates with the creative entrepreneurial spirit behind many of David's projects, like Senior Parks USA and The International Entrepreneurs Association.

> "Some people don't like change, but you need to embrace change if the alternative is disaster."
>
> *- Elon Musk*
> *Tesla, SpaceX*

INSIGHTS AND REFLECTIONS

KEYS TO ENTREPRENEURIAL SUCCESS

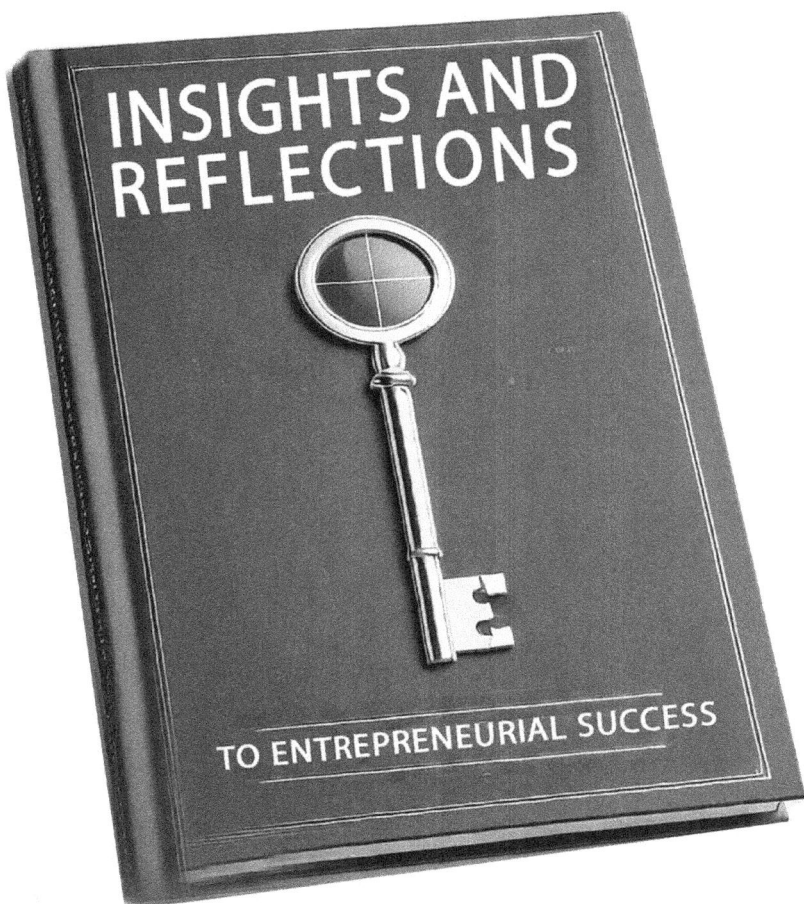

The Power of Origin, Conversion and Purpose

"What if the key to your success lies in understanding three transformative elements—your origin, your pivotal choices, and your driving purpose? Together, they form the foundation, the spark, and the fuel of every entrepreneurial journey."

ORIGIN   CONVERSION   PURPOSE

My journey from Beginnings to Breakthroughs

Every entrepreneur's journey is built on three pillars: origin, conversion, and purpose. Origin is where we start—the early days that shape our values and skills. Our "purpose" is the mission that drives us forward, the reason we keep going. But it's the conversion—the pivotal moment when we make a choice, take a risk, or see things in a new way—that breathes life into that purpose, sharpening it and turning it into a force that guides us through every step."

"In this chapter, I'll take you through my own journey and show you how each of these pillars played a role. My origins laid the foundation, but it was in the conversion moments—the choices to go further, to push past fear and uncertainty—that my "purpose" truly came into focus. For any new entrepreneur, understanding these elements can be the difference between a life of mere ambition and a life of meaningful impact."

Section 1

My Beginnings –

Early Lessons from Humble Origins

My story starts in England. As a boy, I wasn't dreaming of empires or million-dollar ventures; I just wanted enough to explore, to see what was out there. I worked whatever odd jobs I could find, saving every penny I made. At the time, these jobs were not glamorous; they were ordinary, everyday work. But I see now how they formed a foundation, teaching me grit, resourcefulness, and the value of hard work.

"Those were my origins: simple, steady steps. I didn't know it then, but I was building a skill set and a work ethic that would support everything I'd go on to do."

Insight for the Reader: "In the early stages, don't worry if you don't have it all figured out. The basics—like grit, resilience, and staying resourceful—will be your foundation. These small beginnings will serve you well as your purpose unfolds.

Section 2

My First Conversions –

Finding Purpose through Pivotal Choices

The first big shift, my first conversion, came when I decided to leave everything familiar behind and set sail for Canada. It was a risk, and I knew it, but I had to go. Deep down, I had a feeling I couldn't ignore—a pull that told me this was a step I needed to take, even if it meant leaving the world I knew.

Looking back, I realize that my purpose didn't just appear; it emerged gradually, especially in moments where I made hard choices. Canada wasn't just a new place; it was a new beginning for me. I didn't know it yet, but I was making a choice that would shape my mission for years to come.

Insight for the Reader: Conversion moments happen when you're willing to choose change, even when it's uncomfortable. These are the moments when purpose begins to reveal itself, often through risk and courage.

<h2 style="text-align:center">Section 3</h2>

Purpose through Challenge –

How Trials Strengthened My Mission

Over the years, I launched and lost more ventures than I could count. Some thrived, and some failed spectacularly. But every time I faced a setback, I kept going, not because I was after success alone, but because there was something deeper driving me. Each failure, every restart, added clarity to my purpose. I realized that my mission wasn't just about what I could build; it was about what I could offer to others and how I could make an impact.

Failures and challenges test your commitment to purpose. But purpose kept me grounded. It was the fuel behind every venture and every attempt to try again.

Insight for the Reader: Purpose is the anchor that holds you steady through setbacks. If you let your purpose grow with each lesson learned, you'll find that even failures play a role in defining your mission.

Today's entrepreneurial trials look different from those of the past. Entrepreneurs face the challenge of adapting to rapid technological advancements like AI, which can disrupt entire industries almost overnight. At the same time, balancing the demands of profitability with sustainability presents a complex but necessary challenge. Businesses that fail to evolve risk irrelevance, but those that integrate these modern elements into their strategies find themselves better equipped to thrive. Each new obstacle—whether embracing AI, adapting to a gig economy workforce, or pursuing environmental sustainability — offers an opportunity to align your mission with the needs of a rapidly changing world.

Section **4**

Purpose as Influence –

Inspiring Others through My Journey

As my life unfolded, I started to see purpose as something much larger than myself. It wasn't just about my journey anymore; it was about how my experiences could serve others. Through the International Entrepreneur Assoc, I found a way to pass on what I'd learned, helping new entrepreneurs find their own paths.

Purpose isn't meant to stay hidden. When you lead with purpose, you create something others want to be a part of. You don't just build a business—you build a legacy. And when people connect with your story, they feel inspired to find their own purpose.

Insight for the Reader: When you share your purpose, you invite others into your journey. Use your story to empower others and create something lasting.

Globalization of Entrepreneurship: Origin, Conversion and Purpose in a Global Landscape

Today's entrepreneurs are not limited by borders. In a globalized world, purpose, origin, and conversion take on a new dimension, allowing us to think and operate beyond traditional boundaries. Our origins may begin in one place, shaped by local culture and values, but the global landscape gives us access to diverse perspectives, resources, and markets that enrich our entrepreneurial foundations.

Conversion, in this global sense, is the moment we realize that our work can impact not just our immediate community, but people and industries around the world. Purpose becomes more than a personal mission—it becomes a commitment to creating value on a larger scale, with solutions that address global needs and connect us across continents.

In this interconnected era, technology like artificial intelligence (AI) has transformed the way businesses operate, enabling entrepreneurs to access real-time data, automate workflows, and deliver personalized customer experiences at scale. However, these advancements come with challenges: how to use AI responsibly, avoid bias, and ensure it enhances rather than replaces human ingenuity.

Sustainability has also become a key driver of innovation, as consumers increasingly seek eco-friendly products and services. Entrepreneurs who prioritize ethical sourcing, green energy, and reducing waste are not only meeting this demand but are also paving the way for a more sustainable future.

Meanwhile, the gig economy has redefined thel workforce, offering entrepreneurs access to a global pool of talent. While this opens doors to collaboration, it also requires careful management of issues like fair compensation, cultural diversity, and building loyalty in a nontraditional workforce. Globalization allows entrepreneurs to think beyond borders, but it also demands a deeper commitment to ethics, inclusivity, and innovation.

Wrap-Up: Purpose —

The Compass for Every Entrepreneur

Looking back, I can tell you this: purpose is the foundation, the fuel, and the guiding force behind everything worthwhile. It's what keeps you going when times are tough and pushes you to make an impact that matters. You don't need to have it all figured out at the beginning; purpose evolves. But let it be your true north, shaping your path as you grow.

Looking Ahead

Understanding your origin—where you come from and why you started—is a powerful first step. Your story gives you purpose and clarity, but true success often requires going beyond it. To grow, you need the courage to challenge norms and think differently. Let's explore how stepping outside the ordinary can lead to extraordinary breakthroughs.

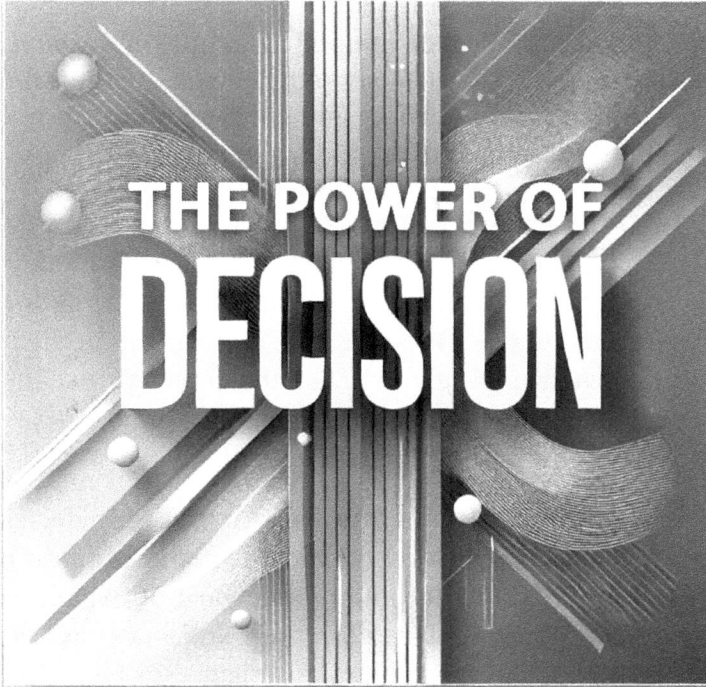

Decisions Define Destinies

As entrepreneurs, we are constantly making decisions. Some are small and seemingly insignificant, like choosing what color to paint an office. Others are monumental, like deciding to pivot a business or invest in a new idea. But what I've learned over the years is that hesitation—the inability to decide—can be far more damaging than making the wrong choice. Indecision keeps you stuck, while action, even imperfect action, moves you forward.

A Framework for Decision-Making

Over the years, I've developed a simple approach to decision-making that has served me well. It's not about perfection; it's about clarity and courage. Here are a few principles I've leaned on:

1. **Define Your Vision:** Before you make any decision, you have to know where you're headed. I always ask myself, "Does this align with my long-term goals?" When I was deciding whether to move from England to Canada, it wasn't just about leaving home. It was about pursuing a dream of building something bigger than myself.

2. **Weigh the Risks and Rewards:** Every decision involves some level of risk. The key is understanding whether the potential reward outweighs the risk. When I invested in the "Nothing Down Real Estate" venture, I knew the risks. But I also knew the potential upside was worth it, and I trusted my ability to navigate challenges.

3. **Listen to Your Gut:** While logic is important, I've found that intuition often knows what the mind doesn't. Some of my best decisions came from trusting that inner voice that said, "Go for it."

4. **Act Decisively:** Once you've gathered the facts and listened to your intuition, act. Don't overthink it. Hesitation kills momentum and erodes confidence.

5. **Learn from the Outcome:** Not every decision will lead to success, but every decision will teach you something. The key is to embrace the lessons and use them to make better choices in the future.

The Importance of Letting Go

One of the hardest parts of decision-making is letting go of the past. Until you close one chapter, you can't fully open the next. I've seen entrepreneurs, including myself, stay stuck in failing ventures or unproductive habits simply because we were afraid to finalize a decision. But here's the truth: holding onto indecision is like trying to sail with an anchor dragging behind you.

When I decided to leave a stable corporate job to pursue my entrepreneurial dreams, it wasn't easy. I had to let go of the security and familiarity of a paycheck. But that final decision—to let go completely—was what allowed me to step fully into my new venture. It's the same for any major decision: until you let go, you'll remain stuck.

Lessons from My Ventures

In my entrepreneurial journey, decisions have been the turning points of my ventures. When I started Senior Parks USA, the idea of developing affordable housing communities for seniors was daunting. The financial risks were significant, and I had to make decisions quickly. But I reminded myself of a simple truth: the best ideas often come with the biggest risks. By staying focused and trusting my instincts, I turned that dream into a reality.

On the flip side, I've made decisions that didn't pan out. The "Start Me Up Auto Product" venture was one of those. I believed in the product, but I didn't adequately consider the market challenges or the need for better capitalization. It was a painful failure, but it reinforced the importance of thorough research and planning before committing to a big decision.

Common Decision Traps

Making decisions can be tricky, and there are common traps that entrepreneurs often fall into. Avoiding these pitfalls can save time, money, and stress:

- **Overthinking:** Spending too much time analyzing can paralyze you. Set a deadline for your decision and stick to it.

- **Fear of Failure:** Failure isn't the end; it's a learning opportunity. Don't let the fear of getting it wrong stop you from acting.

- **Decision Fatigue:** Making too many decisions at once can wear you out. Prioritize the most important ones and delegate the rest.

Practical Exercises for Better Decisions

Here are a few tools to help you make better decisions:

1. **The Decision Checklist:**

    - o Does this align with my vision?
    - o What are the risks, and can I handle them?
    - o What does my gut say?
    - o What's the worst-case scenario, and can I live with it?

2. **The One-Minute Decision Exercise:**

    - o Take 60 seconds to write down your options.
    - o Cross off the ones that don't align with your goals.
    - o Choose the one that feels most aligned and take the first step immediately.

3. **Letting Go Exercise:**

    - o Write down something you've been holding onto that's preventing you from moving forward.
    - o Ask yourself: What's the cost of holding onto this?
    - o Decide on one action to help you let it go, whether it's delegating, selling, or simply walking away.

The "Courage" to Decide

Making decisions isn't easy. Fear of failure, the unknown, or even success can paralyze us. But courage isn't the absence of fear; it's acting despite it. Every successful entrepreneur faces tough, scary decisions. The difference is, they don't let fear stop them.

If you're reading this, you might be facing a tough decision of your own. Maybe it's about starting a new venture, leaving a stable job, or investing in an idea that keeps you awake at night. Whatever it is, remember this: no one ever built a legacy by playing it safe. The power to decide is one of the greatest gifts you have. Use it wisely, but use it.

Final Thoughts

The power of decision is what separates dreamers from doers. It's not about always being right; it's about being willing to step forward and take a chance. As I look back on my life and my ventures, I see a mosaic of decisions—some good, some bad—that have brought me to where I am today. And I wouldn't change a thing.

So, my advice to you is simple: **decide.** *Decide* to take the first step. *Decide* to keep going when it gets tough. *Decide* to let go of what no longer serves you, and bet on yourself, even when no one else will. Because at the end of the day, your life and your success will be defined by the choices you make.

Thinking against the grain:
Lessons from a
Contrarian Entrepreneur

Looking back, I sometimes wonder how different things might have turned out if I'd chosen alternate paths. While I can't go back and rewrite my story, I believe everything happened for a reason, leading me to the lessons I was meant to learn. For those of you walking your own path, here are some ways to look at key moments in a different light. Let these reflections offer you a fresh perspective, one that might lead to an outcome entirely your own.

*Being a contrarian in business goes beyond simply opposing the mainstream; it's a way of seeing the world through a different lens. For me, it meant looking at the overlooked, questioning the so-called 'rules,' and following a hunch even when logic—and sometimes everyone else—told me to think twice. Early on, I realized that if everyone agreed something was impossible, that's where I needed to dig in. I looked for gaps where others saw solid ground, for value where others saw nothing but risk. In one of my ventures, people warned me it wouldn't work—they couldn't see past the flaws to spot the opportunity. But I knew the value was there, hidden beyond the surface issues.

Contrarian thinking means embracing a certain level of discomfort. You have to be willing to stand alone, to go against the prevailing tide, knowing full well that there's a good chance you could fail. But I always believed that in business, playing it safe was often the riskiest choice of all. A contrarian looks at a crowded market and asks, 'What's missing?' They look at trends and ask, 'What's next?' It's about a willingness to make moves that others find unthinkable. At times, this way of thinking has made my journey harder, forcing me to confront unexpected challenges and deep setbacks. But it's also what set my ventures apart and brought me closer to opportunities.

Contrarians don't simply reject the rules; they know when to question them, when to tweak them, and when to create their own. That's the heart of this book—stories of ventures where thinking differently didn't just help me survive; it helped me thrive. If you're reading this, take it as a call to embrace that contrarian within you. Look for the paths no one else notices, trust your intuition over popular advice, and remember that in the world of entrepreneurship, real growth happens just outside the comfort zone.

1. The Leap into the Unknown:
Pursuing a Venture with Limited Resources

When I first considered diving into a new market with minimal capital and scant connections, conventional wisdom would have advised waiting—building a stronger foundation first. But there was something in me that said, *"If you wait too long, the opportunity will be gone."* So, I jumped in.

Contrarian Perspective: What if I had spent time building resources and networks instead? This approach might have offered more security, reducing the strain I faced early on. But I would have missed the experience of rapid problem-solving, learning on my feet, and the thrill of success through sheer resilience. Sometimes, the rush of going for it with limited means is where real growth happens.

2. The Passion-Driven Project:
Prioritizing Purpose Over Profit

One of my ventures was driven more by passion than by profit—a choice that many would caution against. People told me, *"It's business; don't get too attached."* But my gut told me that passion would be what sustained me through the inevitable rough patches, and I held onto it.

Contrarian Perspective: A more pragmatic approach might have been to keep my focus solely on what was profitable, and to let go of ideas that didn't promise immediate returns. However, there's something to be said for finding work that feeds the soul. Purpose can keep us going long after financial incentives have worn thin. If I had focused purely on the numbers, I may not have had the resilience or satisfaction that drove me forward.

Highlight # 1:
The Leap into New Markets

One of my most ambitious ventures involved entering a market with little experience but a lot of passion. Conventional wisdom would say that starting in a new industry demands caution, research, and significant groundwork. Instead, I dove in, driven by excitement and a vision. Looking back, what if I had taken more time to analyze the risks or partnered with someone with expertise in that field? Perhaps the business would have lasted longer. Or perhaps I would have missed out on the wild, inspiring challenges that ultimately pushed me to grow.

Lesson: Sometimes, boldness is its own reward, but pairing it with a bit of research can create a powerful combination.

Highlight # **2**:
Rejecting the "Sure Bet" for Passion

At one point, I faced a decision to pursue a highly profitable opportunity that didn't excite me or continue with a smaller venture that sparked my passion. The "safe" choice was obvious to everyone else, but I couldn't let go of what truly mattered to me. I chose passion over profit, though it was a risky path. **What if** I'd taken the sure bet? Perhaps I'd have made more money—but would I have felt fulfilled? This choice taught me that passion often carries a hidden currency of its own, something that can't be measured in profit alone.

Lesson: Profit alone may keep the lights on, but passion keeps the spirit alive.

Highlight # **3**:
Going Against Expert Advice

In one venture, I was advised repeatedly to scale back and reduce my offerings. Experts claimed I was spreading myself too thin, but I saw potential in each service. I kept expanding despite the warnings. *What if* I had taken their advice and focused on a single offering? I might have developed it faster, perhaps achieving early success. But, as it happened, the diversity of services kept the business interesting for me and allowed it to evolve in unexpected ways.

 Lesson: Experts bring valuable insight, but they don't always know the whole story. Trusting your gut sometimes pays dividends that no advisor can foresee.

*Highlight #*4:
Taking an Emotional Risk

When I acquired a seasonal business on a whim, many people called it impulsive. I was swept up by the charm of the location and the opportunity. Had I taken more time to evaluate the seasonal challenges or listened to warnings about cash flow issues, I might have avoided financial stress. **But what if** I had let caution hold me back? Perhaps I wouldn't have experienced the unique lessons this venture taught me about resilience and adaptation.

Lesson: Emotional risks can be costly, but they often offer lessons that cautious choices don't.

Wrap-Up: Think About This

Reflect on your journey:

- Are you following the crowd, or are you brave enough to challenge conventional wisdom?

- What risks have you avoided that might hold the key to your next breakthrough?

- Where in your business or life can you take a bold, contrarian step?

Looking Ahead

Challenging conventional wisdom is vital for innovation, but today's entrepreneurs also face unique, modern challenges. Balancing these with timeless principles can help you thrive no matter the circumstances. Let's examine how to navigate the complexities of today's world while staying grounded in proven lessons.

> It's not about breaking the rules for the sake of it; it's about seeing the world differently and daring to act on what you see."—
>
> *- David Selley*
> *Entrepreneur, Author*

> "The greatest success
> is not what you achieve,
> but how you help others
> achieve greatness."
>
> *- David Selley*

Modern Challenges,
Timeless Lessons

"Are you ready to uncover the lessons hidden in the chaos of our time? The future isn't shaped by those who follow the rules—it's forged by those who dare to question   them, embrace the unknown, and see opportunity in the challenges others fear"

Entrepreneurship has always been a blend of timeless principles and adapting to the ever-changing world. Resilience, adaptability, and purpose are constants— they've been the foundation of every successful venture

I've ever been part of. But as the world evolves, so do the challenges entrepreneurs face. From the rapid rise of artificial intelligence to the global demand for sustainability and the transformation of the workforce through the gig economy, today's business landscape is unlike anything we've seen before.

I've had the privilege of using one of these transformative technologies—artificial intelligence—while crafting this very book. AI has helped refine the structure, ensure clarity, and organize my decades of experiences into something I hope is both practical and inspiring. It's incredible to see how technology can amplify what we do, and it's a reminder that innovation is not something to fear but something to embrace.

As entrepreneurs, we don't just adapt to these changes— we lead through them. These modern challenges are opportunities in disguise, offering us the chance to rethink, innovate, and thrive.

The Power of AI: Beyond Automation

Artificial intelligence has changed the entrepreneurial game entirely. I've seen firsthand how it can analyze data at levels we couldn't imagine just a few years ago, helping businesses predict trends, optimize operations, and connect with customers on a deeper, more personal level. But AI is more than just a tool for efficiency—it's a tool for innovation.

Of course, with great power comes responsibility. AI brings challenges, like ethical concerns around bias in algorithms and the delicate balance between automation and human touch. For smaller businesses, accessibility can also be a hurdle. But the beauty of AI lies in its versatility. Entrepreneurs who use it thoughtfully can stay true to their values while unlocking its immense potential.

Key Takeaway: Use AI not to replace the human touch but to enhance it, allowing you to connect, innovate, and solve problems in ways that were once unimaginable.

Sustainability: The New Standard

When I first started my journey, sustainability wasn't a buzzword—it wasn't even on the radar. Today, it's a non-negotiable. With climate change and resource depletion becoming undeniable realities, businesses have a responsibility to do more than just turn a profit. Consumers and investors are now demanding eco-friendly practices, from reducing waste to using renewable energy.

For entrepreneurs, this shift is an opportunity to lead the way. By integrating sustainable practices, we can not only differentiate ourselves in the market but also build something lasting—something that serves people and the planet. Whether it's ethical sourcing, circular business models, or designing products that minimize waste, sustainability has the power to drive innovation and customer loyalty.

Key Takeaway: Sustainability isn't just the right thing to do—it's the smart thing to do. Entrepreneurs who embrace it are building the businesses of the future.

The Gig Economy: A Flexible Workforce

The gig economy refers to a labor market characterized by short-term, flexible jobs or freelance work, often facilitated through digital platforms. Instead of traditional full-time employment, workers take on "gigs" or individual tasks, projects, or assignments.

The gig economy has redefined how we think about teams and talent. When I look at platforms like Upwork and Fiverr, I see something remarkable: a global marketplace of skills at your fingertips. For entrepreneurs, this means you can scale faster, tap into specialized expertise, and remain agile in a competitive world.

But working with a gig-based team has its own challenges. Loyalty, cohesion, and fair treatment are all crucial. A team that feels valued will deliver their best work, no matter where they're located. Balancing flexibility with trust is the key to making the gig economy work for you.

Key Takeaway: The gig economy offers incredible opportunities, but success comes from building trust and investing in ethical practices.

The Entrepreneurial Opportunity

If there's one thing I've learned, it's that every challenge holds an opportunity. AI, sustainability, and the gig economy may seem overwhelming at first, but they're also the tools and trends that will shape the next generation of businesses. Entrepreneurs who approach these changes with vision and creativity won't just survive—they'll lead the way.

At the same time, it's important to remember that the core values of entrepreneurship — resilience, adaptability, and purpose—remain as vital today as they were when I started my first venture. The tools may change, but the principles are timeless.

Think About This

- How can AI enhance your business while staying true to your values?

- Where in your operations can sustainability create value for both your customers and your bottom line?

- How can the gig economy help you build a dynamic team, and what steps can you take to ensure fairness and cohesion?

As you reflect on these questions, remember the lessons in this book—and in your experiences—will continue to show up throughout your journey. That's the beauty of repetition: it reinforces what matters most, helping you grow and succeed. Use these modern challenges as stepping stones to something extraordinary.

Looking Ahead

Navigating challenges and applying timeless lessons begins with a clear vision of where you're headed. Visualization has been a cornerstone of my journey— helping me turn ideas into reality. Let me show you how seeing beyond the present can shape your path to success.

"If you work just for money,
you'll never make it,
but if you love what you're doing
and you always put the customer first,
success will be yours."

- Ray Kroc, McDonald's

Seeing beyond...
The Power of Visualization in Building Success

"What if the key to extraordinary success lies not in following the rules, but in questioning them? What if your greatest opportunities are hidden in the ideas everyone else dismisses? To think like a contrarian is to see potential where others see impossibility— and to act on it."

Visualization isn't just a mental exercise; it is the foundation of every venture I've taken on. Before I ever put a plan on paper or called a single supplier, I would sit quietly and picture the end result in vivid detail. I would imagine the product in people's hands, the conversations with customers, the excitement in their eyes. I'd see the storefront, the bustling energy, the faces of people experiencing what I'd built. In my mind, I didn't just see the business—I lived it, breathed it, made it real long before it existed in the world.

Visualization, to me, is a roadmap. When you can see the destination, even in your mind's eye, you have a compass guiding you forward. Every decision becomes clearer because you know exactly what you're aiming for. In one of my ventures, I saw a unique store that hadn't yet been created, a place that blended fine foods and unique products in a way people hadn't experienced before. This vision became my anchor. When doubts crept in or I faced a setback, I returned to that mental picture of what success looked like. The clearer that vision became, the more I trusted that I was on the right path.

But here's the thing—they don't tell you about visualization: it's not enough to simply see the end goal. You have to break it down. When I visualized success, I didn't stop at the big picture. I saw each step along the way. I pictured the early mornings, the hands-on work, the conversations with partners. I envisioned how I'd handle obstacles, how I'd pivot when things didn't go as planned. This isn't daydreaming; it's practical preparation. Visualization isn't just about picturing the glory—it's about rehearsing the grind.

Some people might think visualizing success is a waste of time, just a fantasy. But I've found that it's the opposite. The more detailed my vision, the closer I felt to making it a reality. When you visualize, you're preparing your mind to expect success, training yourself to look for the paths others might miss. And if you don't believe in what you're creating enough to see it clearly, to practically touch it in your mind, why would anyone else believe in it?

So, if you're looking to start something, whether it's your first venture or your tenth, start by seeing it. Picture the small steps and the giant leaps. Visualize the challenges, the setbacks, and yourself overcoming them. Because when you can truly see it, not as a distant dream but as an imminent reality, you're already halfway there.

In each venture, visualization was my starting point. It wasn't just about seeing success; it was about picturing every aspect, the details that would drive me through setbacks. Here are four examples from my journey that show how visualization gave me a clear path forward, even when the road looked uncertain.

1. The Sure Safe Auto Device

When I developed an anti-theft device for cars, I knew I was stepping into a tough market. I visualized people in parking lots, shopping centers, and their own garages, feeling the security that my device could offer. I pictured how their cars would be safe, how they'd feel knowing they were protected. But I also visualized the challenges—the need for rigorous testing, overcoming potential safety concerns, and pitching it to skeptical investors. This mental preparation helped me anticipate hurdles and make the right adjustments early on, even though the venture ultimately faced challenges. Visualization kept me realistic yet driven, even when things didn't turn out as I'd hoped.

2. Sonja's Food & Gifts

Before I even opened the doors to Sonja's, a gourmet food and tea shop, I visualized the entire atmosphere. I pictured customers walking in and experiencing the comforting aroma of tea and fresh pastries, the look of wonder as they browsed shelves filled with curated, high-quality products they couldn't find anywhere else. I saw the lighting, the layout, the conversations with loyal customers who returned because they felt a connection. Every detail I visualized shaped how I set up the shop, from the arrangement of products to the warm customer service. That mental picture became my blueprint, helping me create an experience that kept people coming back for more.

3. The Gourmet Chalet

When I opened a seasonal gourmet deli in Tahoe City, I knew the stakes were high. This emotional venture required grounding, so I visualized bustling holiday crowds, the smell of fresh bread, and skiers stopping in for a warm meal. I also pictured the challenges—cold winter days, unpredictable sales, and the need to make every transaction count. Focusing on the highs and lows kept me centered on the customer experience and the bottom line, helping me stay committed to thriving during the short winter season.

Senior Parks USA

This venture involved creating affordable senior housing communities, a project rooted in more than just profit—it was about making a difference. I visualized seniors moving into comfortable, welcoming homes, the sense of community they'd build, the peace of mind it would bring to their families. I pictured the layout of the communities, the services we'd offer, and the smiles on residents' faces as they settled in. But I also visualized the challenges: the funding needed, the red tape involved, and the amount of personal resilience required to see it through. This vision kept me focused on the impact, guiding every decision I made toward creating something meaningful, even when the hurdles seemed endless.

Visualization was my Map

In each of these ventures, visualization wasn't just a motivator—it was my map. When I could see the end result, even the difficult steps along the way gave me the confidence to move forward. So, when you set out to build something, don't just think about the finish line. Visualize each step, the obstacles you'll face, and the way you'll overcome them. Turn a vision into reality.

Looking Ahead *Visualizing your goals provides clarity, but achieving them often requires collaboration and support. Throughout my life, the power of working with the right people has amplified my success. A mastermind group can provide the accountability, wisdom, and encouragement you need to reach new heights. Let's explore how to build this vital support system.*

"In the end, you're measured not
by how much you undertake,
but by what you finally accomplish."

- Donald Trump
45th and 47th President of the United States
Trump Organization

Mastermind
Your Way to Success:
Finding the Right Group for You

*What if the key to your biggest breakthrough is
not in your own head but in the wisdom of others?
What if the right group could challenge your
thinking, hold you accountable, and push you further
than you thought possible?*

Throughout my entrepreneurial journey, one lesson stands out: you can't succeed in isolation. The people you surround yourself with—the ones who challenge, inspire, and hold you accountable—play a pivotal role in your growth. A mastermind group is one of the most powerful tools to elevate your ideas, overcome obstacles, and create extraordinary results.

What Is a Mastermind?

A mastermind is a group of individuals who come together to support each other in achieving their goals. It's not just a meeting or a casual gathering; it's a structured environment where ideas are exchanged, challenges are tackled, and members hold each other accountable.

Imagine having access to a team of advisors, mentors, and collaborators—all committed to helping you succeed. That's the essence of a mastermind. The collective wisdom, energy, and focus of the group can spark breakthroughs that might take you years to achieve on your own.

The Power of a Mastermind:

- Clarity and Focus: Gain new insights into your goals and challenges.

- Accountability That Drives Action: When you commit to your group, you're more likely to follow through.

- Creative Problem-Solving: Different perspectives often reveal solutions you'd never consider alone.

- Mutual Growth: Helps you learn and grow also.

Why Masterminds Matter

- New Perspectives: Gain insights and solutions you'd never arrive at on your own.

- Accountability That Works: Sharing your goals with a group keeps you moving forward.

- Innovation Through Collaboration: Collective wisdom often leads to creative breakthroughs.

- Networking and Opportunities: Build meaningful connections that open doors you never expected.

In-Person vs. Zoom Meetings: The New Dynamic

In today's world, masterminding has evolved to include both in-person and virtual formats, each offering unique advantages:

The Power of In-Person Meetings

- Stronger Connections: Being face-to-face fosters deeper relationships and trust.

- Body Language: Non-verbal cues often spark understanding and connection.

- Focused Collaboration: In-person settings minimize distractions, allowing for high-impact discussions.

- Serendipity: Casual interactions during breaks or after the session can lead to unexpected ideas or partnerships.

The Advantages of Zoom and Virtual Meetings

- Global Reach: Connect with members from around the world without the need for travel.

- Convenience: Attend meetings from the comfort of your home or office.

- Flexibility: Easier to schedule meetings with participants in different time zones.

- Cost-Effective: Save time and money on travel and venue expenses.

Why Both Are Important

- Combining in-person and virtual masterminds can give you the best of both worlds. In-person meetings build stronger bonds and focus, while Zoom sessions maintain regular communication and allow for diverse, global participation.

How to Find the Right Mastermind for You

Finding or creating a mastermind group tailored to your goals is crucial. Here's how to do it:

1. Get Clear on Your Goals:

   o Are you looking for growth, global connections, or specific problem-solving?

2. Seek Shared Values:

   o Ensure the group's culture aligns with collaboration, trust, and mutual respect.

3. Evaluate the Format:

   o Decide if you prefer in-person meetings, virtual ones, or a combination of both.

4. Check the Member Mix:

   o Look for diversity in skills and industries while ensuring shared commitment.

5. Leverage Technology:

   o Platforms like Zoom make it easy to join or create a group, especially if participants are geographically dispersed.

6. Test Before You Commit:

   o Attend a trial meeting to gauge the group's energy, focus, and alignment with your needs.

7. Build Your Own:

   o If you can't find a group that fits, take the lead. Craft a hybrid model with both in-person and virtual sessions to maximize flexibility and impact.

Think About This

- Do you thrive more in face-to-face interactions, or do you appreciate the global reach of virtual meetings?

- How can you integrate both formats to create a mastermind that fits your lifestyle and goals?

- Are you surrounding yourself with people who inspire and challenge you, or do you need to expand your network?

My Closing Thoughts

Masterminding isn't just a tool—it's a mindset. Whether in person or online, the power of collective wisdom can transform your journey. It's not just about the format; it's about the people, the insights, and the shared energy that propel you toward your goals.

Take the leap. Whether it's a handshake over coffee or a wave through a screen, your next big idea might come from the connections you make.

Looking Ahead

Collaboration can elevate your journey, but personal growth also depends on feeding your mind with the right knowledge. The books you read shape your thinking, sharpen your skills, and inspire new ideas. Let's dive into why reading the right books is one of the most valuable habits you can develop.

Feed Your Mind:
The Importance of
Reading the *Right* Books

*Doorways to new ideas, strategies, and perspectives....
What if the next book you read could change the way
you think, solve problems and grow your business?*

If I had to pinpoint one habit that has consistently fueled my growth as an entrepreneur, it would be reading. The right books have a way of unlocking ideas, revealing strategies, and teaching lessons that can transform the way you think and work. Every great book is a shortcut—a chance to absorb someone else's lifetime of experience in just a few hours.

As an entrepreneur, you're constantly faced with challenges, decisions, and opportunities. Books provide the tools you need to navigate them. They teach you how to problem-solve, how to lead, and how to turn obstacles into stepping stones. They expand your mind, refine your strategies, and remind you that you're not alone on this journey.

Why Reading the Right Books Matters

- **Expand Your Knowledge**: Books offer insights from industries, leaders, and innovators beyond your immediate circle.

- **Practical Solutions**: Whether it's marketing, leadership, or finance, the right book can provide step-by-step guidance.

- **Inspiration and Motivation**: A well-written story of triumph can reignite your passion and push you to keep going.

- **Refined Decision-Making**: The more you know, the better equipped you are to make informed, strategic choices.

How to Find the Right Books for Your Needs

Not all books are created equal, and finding the right ones can make a world of difference. Here's how to identify the books that will have the greatest impact on your journey:

1. **Define Your Goals**:
   - What challenges are you facing right now? Look for books that address those specific areas—be it scaling your business, improving leadership skills, or mastering finances.

2. **Seek Recommendations**:
   - Ask successful entrepreneurs and mentors what books influenced them. Personal referrals often uncover hidden gems.

3. **Explore Thought Leaders**:
   - Follow the authors, speakers, and industry experts who are at the forefront of your field. Their books are likely packed with valuable insights.

4. **Balance Depth and Breadth**:
   - Read books that deepen your expertise in your current focus but also explore topics outside your comfort zone to broaden your perspective.

5. **Read Reviews and Summaries**:
   - Don't judge a book by its cover. Look at

reviews and summaries to see if the content matches your needs before committing.

6. **Create a Reading List**:

   o Plan your reading in advance, prioritizing the books that align with your goals for the year.

7. **Be Willing to Abandon Books**:

   o If a book isn't resonating or providing value, don't be afraid to put it down and move on.

Think About This

- Are you intentionally choosing books that align with your current challenges and goals, or are you reading aimlessly?

- How can you balance reading for inspiration with reading for practical strategies?

- What is the one book that has most influenced your entrepreneurial journey so far? What's next?

My Closing Thoughts

Throughout my life, books have been more than a source of knowledge—they've been my mentors, my problem-solvers, and my inspiration. Reading isn't just about gathering information; it's about transforming the way you think and approach the world.

Finding the right books isn't just a task—it's an investment in yourself. The lessons you'll uncover, the ideas you'll spark, and the strategies you'll gain will more than repay the time and effort you put in.

Make reading a priority, and choose books that challenge you, teach you, and push you forward. You'll be amazed at how much growth is just a page away.

Looking Ahead

The knowledge you gain from books has the power to shape your thinking and transform your journey, but it's what you do with that knowledge that truly counts. Repetition and consistency are the keys to turning what you've learned into real, lasting success. Let's explore why revisiting and refining your practices is essential for building a foundation that stands the test of time.

> "Constantly think about how you
> could be doing things better
> and keep questioning yourself."
>
> *- Elon Musk*
> *CEO and Technoking of Tesla / CEO and CTO of SpaceX*
> *Co-Chair Dept. of Government Efficiency (DOGE)*

The Power of Repetition: Why We Revisit the Same Lessons

"What if the secret to mastering anything isn't in discovering something new, but in revisiting the familiar—again and again? Repetition isn't just redundancy; it's the quiet force that transforms understanding into wisdom, and action into mastery. The question is: Are you willing to embrace it?"

When I started writing this book, I had one goal in mind: to share the lessons I've learned in a way that sticks with you. And I'll let you in on a little secret—repetition is the name of the game. If you've noticed certain themes popping up again and again throughout these chapters, that's not by accident. It's because the most important lessons in entrepreneurship—and in life—are worth revisiting, over and over.

You see, repetition is more than just a teaching method. It's a way of ingraining knowledge so deeply that it becomes second nature. Whether it's building resilience, adapting to change, or staying true to your purpose, these lessons aren't one-and-done ideas. They're truths that demand reflection, practice, and, yes, repetition.

Why Repetition Matters

Think about the first time you learned something new—whether it was riding a bike, playing a musical instrument, or even starting a business. Did you master it the first time? Of course not. You had to try, fail, and try again. That's the power of repetition. It transforms what feels awkward and unfamiliar into something instinctive and natural.

In my own journey, I've learned that revisiting the same principles is essential for growth. Every time I've faced a challenge—whether it was launching a new venture, navigating failure, or stepping into an unknown market—I found myself drawing on the same core ideas. Resilience. Creativity. Adaptability. These aren't lessons you learn once and leave behind. They're lessons you carry with you, sharpening them with every experience.

How Repetition Shapes Success

In business, repetition is everywhere. Think about marketing campaigns: you don't just tell your story once and expect the world to remember it. You tell it again and again until it sticks. Or consider your daily habits—those small, repeated actions that, over time, define who you are and what you achieve.

The same applies to the lessons in this book. I've repeated themes intentionally because I know how crucial they are. You might find yourself reading about resilience in one chapter and then encountering it again later. That's because resilience isn't just one part of the entrepreneurial journey—it's woven into every stage. The same goes for purpose, adaptability, and learning from failure. These aren't isolated ideas; they're the threads that tie everything together.

The Role of Repetition in This Book

If I've done my job, this book isn't just something you read once and put on a shelf. It's a tool you can return to whenever you need clarity, inspiration, or a reminder of why you started. The repetition you've encountered isn't redundancy, it's reinforcement. I want these lessons to stay with you, to come to mind when you're facing a tough decision or a new challenge.

My Own Lessons Through Repetition

I've lived through decades of entrepreneurship, and let me tell you, the same lessons have shown up time and time again. When I launched my first business, I thought I needed a completely different set of skills than when I tried my second or third venture. But the truth is, the core principles remained the same. It wasn't until I started recognizing the patterns—seeing those lessons repeated in my own life—that I truly began to understand their power.

Embracing Repetition in Your Own Journey

As you move forward in your journey, I encourage you to embrace repetition. Revisit the chapters that resonate most with you. Write down the lessons that stand out. And when you face challenges, ask yourself: what's the core principle here? Chances are, it's something you've already learned—something worth repeating.

Think About This:

- What lessons from this book do you see repeating in your own life or business?

- How can you use repetition to reinforce the habits, skills, and mindsets that lead to success?

- Are you willing to revisit what you've learned—both here and in your own experiences—to uncover deeper insights?

David's Closing Words:

"Repetition isn't redundancy; it's refinement. It's how you turn ideas into action, action into habits, and habits into success. So, if you've felt like I've repeated myself a few times in these pages, good. That means the lessons are sinking in. Keep coming back to them, and they'll serve you well—just as they've served me."

Looking Ahead

Consistency and repetition form the backbone of success, but so does reflection. Taking the time to look back allows you to understand what's worked, what hasn't, and how to move forward with clarity. Now, let's tie it all together and reflect on your journey to prepare for the next chapter.

"I could either watch it happen or be a part of it."

- *Elon Musk*
Tesla, SpaceX

> "We must have a theme, a goal,
> a purpose in our lives.
> If you don't know where you're aiming,
> you don't have a goal."
>
> *- Mary Kay Ash, Mary Kay Cosmetics*

Final Chapter:

Reflecting on Your Entrepreneurial Journey

"Every challenge carries the seeds of innovation. The entrepreneur's job is to find them, nurture them, and let them grow into opportunities." -- David Selley

Think About This – Final Reflect

1. How has your origin shaped your entrepreneurial mindset and values?

2. What pivotal decisions or "conversion moments" have most influenced your path so far?

3. How clear is your purpose, and how does it drive your daily actions and long-term goals?

4. Are you taking enough bold risks, or have you become too comfortable with the familiar?

5. When was the last time you questioned a rule or trend and found an opportunity others missed?

6. How well are you balancing passion and practicality in your ventures?

7. Are you leveraging modern tools like AI or digital platforms to scale your business effectively?

8. In what ways could sustainability become an advantage for your business or personal brand?

9. How are you using the gig economy to expand your reach while maintaining an ethical approach?

10. Have you learned to embrace failure as a tool for growth, or does the fear of failure hold you back?

11. How often do you step outside your comfort zone to explore new opportunities?

12. Are you focusing on building a business, a legacy, or both?

13. What story will your journey tell others about resilience, innovation, and purpose?

14. How can you refine your vision to align with both timeless principles and modern challenges?

15. If you were to start over today, what would you do differently, and why?

16. How can you create a daily habit of revisiting the core lessons you've learned from this book and your own experiences?

17. Are there recurring patterns or challenges in your entrepreneurial journey that you need to address differently?

18. Which area of your life or business would benefit most from intentional repetition—marketing, leadership, or personal growth?

19. How do you balance learning new skills with refining and repeating what you already know?

20. What one lesson from this book will you commit to practicing repeatedly until it becomes second nature?

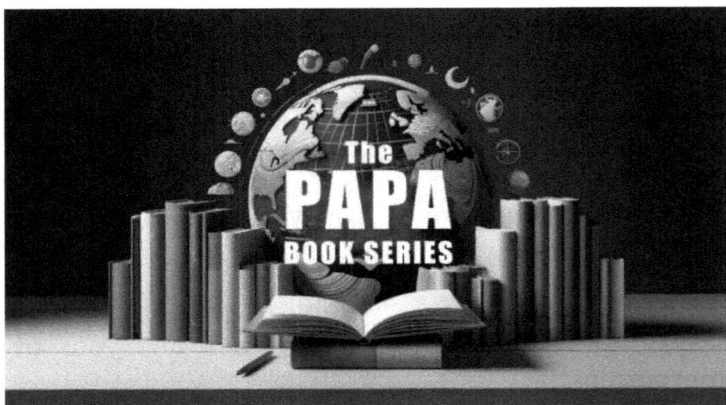

SERIES TITLES AVAILABLE NOW:

PAPA #1: The Boy in England and Growing Up Tough
is a tale of resilience and survival from
David's early days in England.

PAPA #2: The Young Man in Canada provides a look at
his transformative years in Canada, filled with personal
and professional growth.

**PAPA #3: The Businessman and Entrepreneur in the
USA** chronicles David's entry into the business world
and his entrepreneurial adventures in the United States.

PAPA #4: The Entrepreneur: PAPAS Secret #4 takes a
deep dive into his entrepreneurial mindset and the
lessons learned from building businesses.

Continued on next page

TITLES COMING SOON:

PAPA #5: Three Lives, Three Lands
A condensed journey through David Selley's life in England, Canada, and the USA

PAPA #6: Married – The Four Seasons of Marriage reflects on the evolving phases of marriage over 65+ years, from spring to winter.

PAPA #7: How Is Your Relationship?
(How to Stay Married 65+ Years)

PAPA #8: The Father David's journey as a father, filled with challenges, love, and important lessons.

PAPA #9: The Grandfather – Leaving a Legacy is a heartwarming tribute to family and the importance of passing down wisdom and values.

PAPA #10: Health, Wealth & Happiness
(You Can Have All Three)
is a guide to achieving balance and abundance in life.

PAPA #11: The Investor – Nothing Down Real Estate... Yes! It Works presents proven strategies for real estate investing without upfront costs.

PAPA #12: The Famous 50 Book Series is an exciting global vanity publishing project, connecting famous people across industries at *www.famous50.com.*

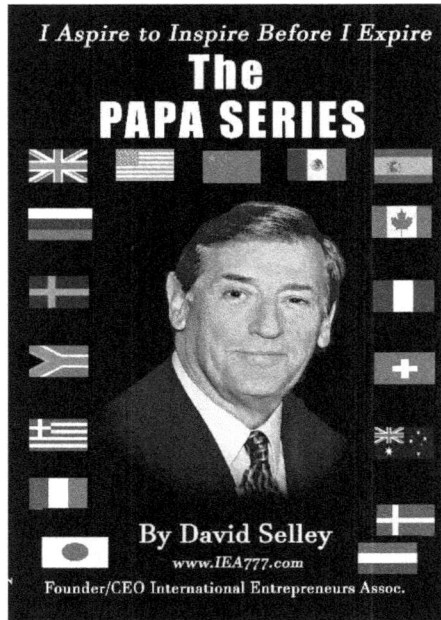

I Aspire to Inspire Before I Expire

The PAPA SERIES

By David Selley
www.IEA777.com
Founder/CEO International Entrepreneurs Assoc.

A celebration of
David Selley's
extraordinary journey across three continents,
The Papa Book Series' chronicles a lifetime of
resilience, entrepreneurship, and heartfelt
stories. Each book is a standalone chapter in an
inspiring legacy, brought together in this
remarkable series.

David's FAVORITE Quotes

Mindset
"You can IF you think you can." – Zig Ziglar

Leadership
"Ask not what your country can do for you...
but what you can do for your country." – John F. Kennedy

Personal Development
"Change your thoughts and you change your world."
– Norman Vincent Peale

Integrity
"Try not to become a man of success.
Rather become a man of value." – Albert Einstein

Self-Belief
"Whatever the mind can conceive and believe,
it can achieve." – Napoleon Hill

Innovation
"The best way to predict the future
is to create it." – Peter F. Drucker

Critical Thinking
"People with polarized opinions will only educate
themselves to their level of ignorance." – David Selley

Practical Wisdom
"Never take advice from someone who has not
done what they are talking about." -- David Selley

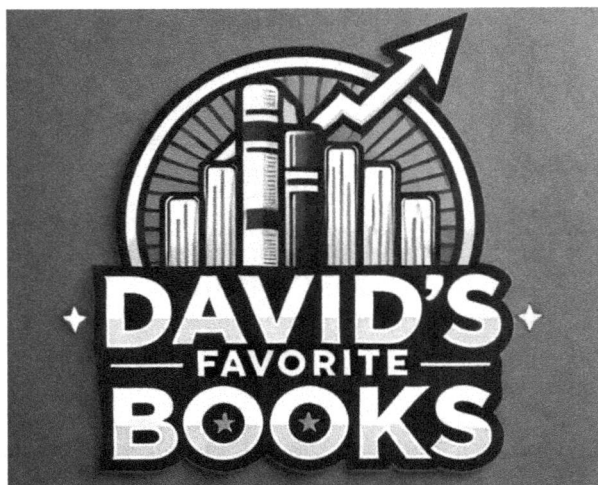

"How to Win Friends and Influence People"
by Dale Carnegie

"The Magic of Thinking Big"
by David J. Schwartz

"Think and Grow Rich"
by Napoleon Hill

"The Power of Positive Thinking"
by Norman Vincent Peale

"The Power of Focus"
by Jack Canfield, Mark Victor Hansen, and Les Hewitt

David's Favorite Books - *Continued*

"The Aladdin Factor"
by Jack Canfield and Mark Victor Hansen

"Innovation and Entrepreneurship"
by Peter F. Drucker

"Secrets of Power Negotiating"
by Roger Dawson

"See You at the Top"
by Zig Ziglar

"Live Your Dreams"
by Les Brown

The Art of Exceptional Living"
by Jim Rohn

The Art of the Deal
Donald J. Trump
45th & 47th President of the United States

**"Maximum Achievement:
Strategies and Skills That Will Unlock
Your Hidden Powers"**
by Brian Tracy

"The 21 Irrefutable Laws of Leadership"
by John C. Maxwell

About the Author

David Selley

David Selley was born in post-war England, where he spent his formative years navigating both hardship and resilience. His story, *"Papa #1,"* recounts his life up to age 15, when he departed for Canada in search of new opportunities. Through vivid storytelling, David shares the challenges and experiences that shaped his early years, offering a unique glimpse into a time of struggle, growth, and hope for a brighter future.

My Creed
By Dean Alfange

*A powerful declaration of
self-reliance, entrepreneurship and personal freedom.*

I do not choose to be a common man,
It is my right to be uncommon … if I can,
I seek opportunity … not security.
I do not wish to be a kept citizen.
Humbled and dulled by having the
State look after me.
I want to take the calculated risk;
To dream and to build.
To fail and to succeed.
I refuse to barter incentive for a dole;
I prefer the challenges of life
To the guaranteed existence;
The thrill of fulfillment
To the stale calm of Utopia.
I will not trade freedom for beneficence
Nor my dignity for a handout
I will never cower before any master
Nor bend to any threat.
It is my heritage to stand erect.
Proud and unafraid;
To think and act for myself,
To enjoy the benefit of my creations
And to face the world boldly and say:
This, with God's help, I have done.

*All this is what it means to be an
"Entrepreneur."*

-Acknowledgements-

Gratitude

FOR YOUR INFLUENCE

To the individuals listed below who I have
been privileged to meet personally, I would like
to publicly say "thank you" for the inspiration
I received from meeting you. That inspiration
has deeply impacted my life and success.
With appreciation -- David Selley

Robert Allen
Nothing Down Real Estate and Author
I bought his "nothing down" book and just did it.
Later on I was grateful to be on his national
infomercials and featured in his 2nd Chancers book.
www.robertallen.com

Foster Brooks
I had the pleasure of sharing 3-4 first-class flights
with the comic Foster from JFK to LAX. He was
genuinely funny and sincere, effortlessly entertaining
the first-class cabin with his quick wit. On one occasion,
I even picked up his luggage. Great memories!

Acknowledgements – *continued*

Les Brown
Famous Motivational Speaker
We met at a function in Atlanta, and I have been inspired by his words ever since.
www.lesbrown.com

George Carlin
A close neighbor on the island in Westlake Village, CA. George had a challenging intellect and a brilliant mind.

William (Bill) Chaplin
is a beautiful example of a "true" entrepreneur. At the age of 18 he defied traditional customs and pursued his dream. He now builds high performance racing cars experiencing a multitude of class wins and national championship honours. If you need a custom car, contact Bill.
www.empireracingcars.com

Prince Charles, Now King of England
Then Prince Charles was the patron of the Royal Bath & West Show in Somerset England. We met at the VIP tent when celebrating Queen Elizabeth's Silver Jubilee. A treasured and inspirational memory.

Rich DeVos, Founder Amway Corporation
Rich offered to help my family during a critical medical emergency. As profit sharing Direct Distributors, I will never forget his kindness. A truly remarkable man who created opportunity for millions and a great company.
www.amway.com

Acknowledgements– *continued*

Elton Gallegly
Thirteen Term California Congressman
Elton was directly responsible for arranging an emergency medical evacuation for our Veteran son from Germany to Texas. I will be eternally grateful for that!

Deborah Gardner
Mrs. Arizona in 2020 and Mrs. America in 2022
is a renowned entrepreneur, author, professional aquatic swimmer, and keynote motivational speaker. She delivers powerful messages globally.
www.iamdeborahg.com

Steve Harrison
Internationally Acclaimed Media and
Personal Development Expert
Steve's powerful guidance and vast media background are guiding me through the launch of my book series. I am grateful for his wisdom and knowledge.
www.steveharrison.com

Mark Victor Hansen
Co-author - The Chicken Soup Book Series
(500 million copies sold!)
A powerful thought leader and transformational thinker, you have taught me how to focus on meaningful story telling. Plus, I loved being part of your exciting Enlightened Millionaire program.
www.markvictorhansen.com

Acknowledgements – *continued*

Robert Kiyosaki
Your financial wisdom, particularly in
Rich Dad Poor Dad, has shaped my financial strategies.
Thank you for that!   - *www.richdad.com*

Carol Lawrence
At 92, this famous and vibrant Broadway star, best
known for her iconic role as Maria in *West Side Story*
and numerous appearances, including seven at the
White House, continues to inspire me. She remains
sharp and down-to-earth despite her polished career.
It has been my pleasure to assist her in many ways and
she continues to inspire me with her wit, charm,
energy and positive attitude.

Ron LeGrand
Real Estate Guru
On a fishing trip to Alaska Ron gave me some great
advice "scratch the barnacles' off your brain and release
yourself to YOUR future. That was a very powerful
message from a guy who knows a lot about real estate.
I appreciate his valuable mentorship!
www.ronlegrand.com

Bob Proctor
Great Thought Leader and
Personal Development Expert
I met Bob at an NSA event in Phoenix. He gave me
one piece of great advice that I will never forget.
"Don't let negativity into your life"
That is wonderful advice for everyone!
www.proctorgallagherinstitute.com

Acknowledgements– *continued*

Jim Rohn
Internationally acclaimed Business and Personal Development Speaker

I was on Jim's last call the day before he died from pulmonary respiratory failure. A remarkable man who has helped millions. – *www.jimrohn.com*

Mickey Rooney

Mickey lived a few doors away from us on the island in West Lake Village, California. We often exchanged pleasantries and frequent visits to the pizza parlor.

Donald Trump
President of the United States

I met Donald at a Jeff Kaller event in Orlando. He said one thing to me that has changed my life. "When you come up with an idea, pull the trigger immediately". That is what I do now! He sent my wife and I a beautiful card for our 60th wedding anniversary. A true entrepreneur and patriot!

Bud Westmore

Bud was one of the famous Westmore brothers from Universal Studios, also a devoted Anglophile. His Encino home reflected British charm, complete with a knight in armor. During lunch at his studio, he showed me the Mermaid and Psycho props. His love for England was clear in our long conversations.

Christian Yelich

Our grandkids and Christian played together at
family parties when we lived in Westlake Village, CA.
Now, a famous MVP and Allstar baseball player.
A true inspiration for me and millions of kids.

Thank you for sharing your knowledge

*"Though we have not met personally, I want to express
my gratitude to the following individuals for their
insights and wisdom, which have been invaluable to me in
accomplishing this book series. Thank you for sharing
your knowledge with the world."*

Dale Carnegie	John Maxwell
Jack Canfield	Norman Vincent Peale
Peter Drucker	Julia Roberts
Roger Dawson	Tony Robbins
Napoleon Hill	Zig Ziglar

Contact David Selley
through www.*DavidSelley.net*
to obtain information about volume
discounts, The Step-by-Step Coaching
Programs, licensing partnership
opportunities, speaker availability.

Three lives - three countries

Regional - National – International

International Entrepreneurs Association

We provide global product distribution and entrepreneurial training through our network of Executive Directors worldwide. Though our business model is new, it is rich in experience, offering a fresh, innovative approach to global business. Our world-class team is driven by need, not greed, with a mission to help marginalized entrepreneurs reach their fullest potential. We aim to serve humanity, leaving a legacy of progress, personal growth, and upholding the highest standards of integrity and core values.

www.IEA777.com

Senior Parks Project

The U.S. faces a critical shortage of affordable senior housing, and Senior Parks USA aims to address this with a national chain of 100-acre parks featuring small, ergonomically designed manufactured homes for seniors. Over the next decade, the plan is to offer dignified, affordable housing to millions of seniors.

www.seniorparksusa.com

The One Day Event for Seniors
Music, Moods & Memories

The One Day Event hosted by **Long Live Seniors** is a unique, interactive experience designed to enrich the lives of seniors by offering valuable resources, expert guidance, and opportunities to connect with others in their community. Focused on promoting health, wellness, and longevity, this event is a one-stop opportunity for seniors and their families to learn, engage, and be inspired.

Event Overview

The One Day Event offers a full day of workshops, seminars, and activities tailored to the needs and interests of seniors. The event is designed to empower seniors by giving them the tools and knowledge they need to live longer, healthier, and more fulfilling lives.

www.LongLiveSeniors.com

MARR**I**ED

David & Sonja
SELLEY

65 Years of Love and Partnership

With over 65 years of marriage, we've discovered that love is a daily decision. Our Married Program provides proven tools to help couples navigate challenges, resolve conflicts, and strengthen their bond. Using the powerful 95-5 and 1-10 techniques, you'll learn how to solve any problem and communicate effectively. Plus, uncover the 10 simple questions that can transform your relationship and deepen your connection. Whether you're rekindling the spark or building a stronger foundation, this program offers a roadmap for lasting love and harmony. Start your journey today and create your own enduring love story.

www.happylifeexpert.com

© 2016

Famous 50 Publishing Series

The Famous 50 Publishing Series offers professionals in over 100 industries the chance to join an exclusive first edition book, featuring 50 top performers. With a 4-page spread for your bio and contact details, this vanity publication is a powerful promotional tool. Gain global exposure and prestige while showcasing your expertise alongside high achievers.

www.famous50.com

Join Today
International Entrepreneurs Association
(IEA) and Get Started for Free

As a member of the IEA, you'll gain access to a community of like-minded entrepreneurs, exclusive webinars, and my personal video series sharing the secrets to building a successful business.
Plus, as a special bonus, you'll receive
***Foundations of Entrepreneurship* (a $97 value)**
absolutely free to kickstart your journey.

Go to **www.IEA777.com**
And sign up while everything is fresh in your mind.

I've walked the path you are about to take—through failure, success, and everything in between. Whether you are just starting, growing your business, or dreaming of global impact, I've created programs to meet you where you are.

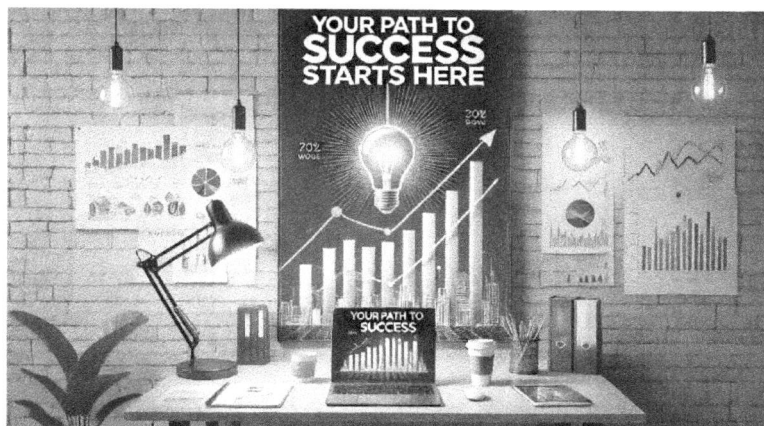

Here's the
Big Deal:

Purchase *Advanced Strategies for Growth* or
Mastering Global Entrepreneurship, and
you will get Foundations of Entrepreneurship
included for free!

Go for the full experience with
Mastering Global Entrepreneurship,
and you'll get all three programs —
because success is best built on a
strong foundation.

This is your moment to step into your potential.
Let me guide you to the entrepreneurial success
you've always dreamed of.

Step by Step Programs

"Building Your Business Plan"
Take Your Business Plan
to the Next Level

The Entrepreneur's Journey:
Step-by-Step Programs
Inspired by David Selley's Legacy

Transform the insights from this book into a complete entrepreneurial roadmap. David Selley's exclusive programs provide practical tools, essential education, and actionable strategies for every stage of your entrepreneurial journey. Choose the path that matches your goals:

Tier 1:
Foundations of Entrepreneurship
For Aspiring Entrepreneurs

Lay the groundwork for your entrepreneurial success. This beginner-friendly program teaches you how to validate your business idea, understand your target market, and create a simple yet effective business plan. You'll also learn:

- **Financial Basics:** Budgeting, funding your idea, and managing cash flow.

- **Market Research:** How to identify industries and niches that align with your skills and passion.

- **Resilience Building:** Tools for overcoming fear, failure, and self-doubt.

- This self-paced course includes worksheets, a risk assessment template, and a personal development checklist to get you started right away.

Value-Packed Price: $97

Tier 2:

Advanced Strategies for Growth
For Growing Entrepreneurs

Level up your business with proven strategies for scaling and growth. This program focuses on:

- **Scaling Your Business:** How to expand operations while maintaining quality.

- **Marketing Strategies:** Build your brand, attract your ideal customers, and create a loyal audience.

- **Financial Mastery:** Advanced budgeting, profit forecasting, and funding options.

- **Leadership Skills:** Managing teams, partnerships, and fostering a growth-oriented culture. You'll receive access to group Q&A sessions, a financial planning workbook, and tools to refine your business plan for long-term success.

Value-Packed Price: $297

Tier 3:
Mastering Global Entrepreneurship For Visionary Entrepreneurs

Become a global leader with tools and strategies for entering international markets and building worldwide connections. This comprehensive program includes:

- **Global Expansion:** Step-by-step guidance on researching and entering new markets.

- **Cross-Cultural Success:** Navigating cultural differences and building international relationships.

- **Advanced Financial Strategies:** Managing currency risks, international taxes, and global logistics.

- Exclusive Access to David's IEA Program: Insights, frameworks, and case studies tailored for global entrepreneurs. You'll also gain access to webinars, a private online mastermind group, and templates for global market research, trade compliance, and business scaling.

Value-Packed Price: $997

TAKE CONTROL
OF YOUR ENTREPRENEURIAL JOURNEY

Each program is designed with actionable steps, real-world tools, and David Selley's decades of entrepreneurial wisdom to ensure your investment delivers results. Whether you are just starting or ready to scale globally, there's a program tailored for you.

I'd Love to Hear from You!

As entrepreneurs, we know the value of learning from one another. I've poured my heart and soul into this book, drawing from decades of experience to make it as meaningful and practical as possible. But I also know there's always room to grow, and that's where you come in.

Your journey is unique, and your insights are invaluable — not just to me but to the entire entrepreneurial community. I'd love to hear your thoughts: What inspired you? What challenged you? What could have been done differently to serve you better?

To make sharing your feedback simple, I've set up a quick survey. It's easy to fill out, and your responses will help shape future editions and projects. Plus, it's an opportunity to connect, collaborate, and continue the conversation.

How to Participate

1. **Visit the Survey:**
   Please go to www.iea777-survey.com to share your thoughts.

2. **Answer a Few Questions:**
   The survey is short—just a few questions about your experience with this book.

3. **Shape the Future:**
   Your feedback will help refine this work and inspire new ideas to better serve entrepreneurs like you.

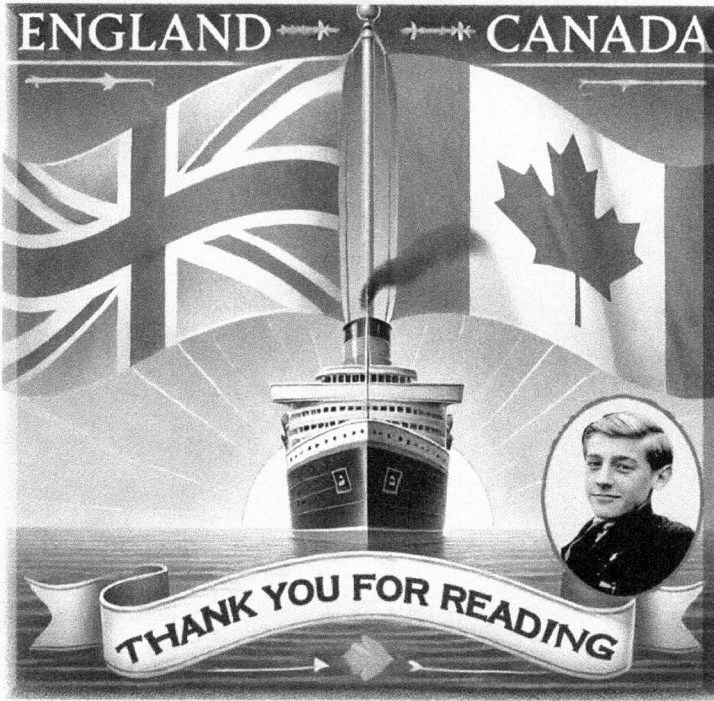

If you enjoyed this book, be sure to explore the rest of the *PAPA Book Series*. Each book offers a unique perspective on David's remarkable life and invaluable lessons on entrepreneurship, family, and success. Stay tuned for more inspiring titles to come!